20/12/16

The Journey

Robert + Betty,

I hope you enjoy
this !

All my

Richard xx

The Journey

Spirituality, Pilgrimage, Chant

J RICHARD SMITH

Royalties will be donated to the charity
Womb Transplant UK

DARTON · LONGMAN + TODD

First published in 2016 by
Darton, Longman and Todd Ltd
1 Spencer Court
140–142 Wandsworth High Street
London SW18 4JJ

ISBN 978-0-232-53232-6

A catalogue record for this book is available from the British Library.

Designed and produced by Judy Linard

Printed and bound in Great Britain by Bell and Bain Ltd, Glasgow

'From where the Western seas gnaw at the coast of Iona.
To the death in the desert,
the prayer in forgotten places by the imperial column.
From such ground springs that which forever renews the earth,
though it is forever denied'
T S Eliot

Dedication

This book is dedicated to my wife Deborah and my four children, Cameron, Victoria, Madeleine and Lara who have been dragged to many an unwelcome site or worse left behind when I have gone off in pursuit of yet another long distance walk.

Contents

*Noel print run – you will both
be in Love,*

Acknowledgements

I wish very much to thank the Revd Gary Bradley, Vicar of Little Venice, London for his wonderful friendship, travel companionship, wise counsel and advice. I wish to express my heartfelt thanks to the Revd Dr Andrew Wakeham-Dawson, my ace walking companion who has, along with his wife Suzie given much advice on this book. My thanks go to the wonderful John Harrison, literary agent for his advice and great efforts to find a suitable publisher, and to David Moloney, great editor and publisher at Darton, Longman and Todd Ltd, his input has been vitally important. I thank Robert Chandler for his great companionship – we Glaswegians have had many a laugh. My gratitude is also extended to Professor Alan Richardson for his help, friendship and comments on this text. Also to Neil Huband for his constructive criticism which altered the final text. I would also like to express my gratitude to Rodena Kelman for her superb organisation of the trips and for typing the first and second transcripts of this document. I am very grateful to my research doctorate fellow Ben Jones for his computer competence and assistance and great help with editorial corrections. I also wish to thank Shelby Bennett, and Tracey Scott for their administrative and typing help. My thanks go to my wife, Deborah and my four children who have been dragged footsore to many a religious site.

I wish to thank Metropolitan Kallistos for his introduction to the Abbott at the Monastery of St John the Divine on Patmos, and to three of the friends of Mount Athos, Dimitri Conomos, Simon Jennings and Graham Speake for their support. I also wish to thank Father Anthony Speakman of the Parish of Little Venice for his advice and blessings on this project and also for reading one of the penultimate versions of this text. Thank you also to Petroula and Kostas Stergiou, Proprietors of the Petra Hotel, Patmos, and their son Christos. They helped so much to create an environment where I could work long hours and almost finish this book.

I am very much in debt to my sister Alison, who has read the text, and made many helpful suggestions. You can be very grateful for her editorial suggestions. She has taken part in many of the walks and alternately kept me or my children to allow me to finish this project. When she finished editing she spontaneously wrote a one page piece on her woman's perspective which I have included. Catrina Donegan has spent much time looking after my children thus facilitating these journeys and for this and much else I am extremely grateful. For the final gasp of this project many thanks to my parents, Diana and the sadly late Irvine Smith, for allowing me a few days writing time where I was well fed and watered in the wilds of Scotland's West Highlands.

Finally, and I only wish I could name her, but of course cannot due to reasons of confidentiality, I would like to thank one of my patients who delivered clarity to me as to who this book is intended for. I said to her: 'I am not sure whether I am talking to my friends or my patients.' She said: 'Surely you are talking to somebody like me! You have known me for many years, we are on first name terms, I am your patient but we don't socialise together.' That intervention proved pivotal. My sincere thanks go to you!

About the author

My name is Richard Smith. I was born in Falkirk in Scotland. I was educated at Dollar Academy and thereafter Glasgow University where I qualified with a medical degree in 1982. After this I undertook a thesis on the interaction of viruses and cervical cancer graduating with an MD from Glasgow University. I am a Fellow of the Royal College of Obstetricians and Gynaecologists and for the last twenty-eight years have lived and worked in London, with the exception of a brief sabbatical in New York. I currently work as a gynaecological surgeon at Imperial College NHS Trust, London, based at Hammersmith, Queen Charlotte's and Charing Cross hospitals. I also hold an Adjunct Associate Professorship at New York University School of Medicine.

My current three main professional interests are in communication, cancer survivorship, and fertility-sparing surgery for women with cancer and serious benign conditions. I am also highly interested in the possibilities of fertility restoration via womb transplantation for women who have been born without or lost their womb. Hence royalties from this book are going to Womb Transplant UK charity of which I am the Chairman. (Charity number: 1138559.)

Other books by this author

For patients:

1.	J R Smith, G Del Priore, *Women's Cancers: Pathways to Living* (Imperial College Health Press, 2015).

2. J R Smith, G Del Priore, *Women's Cancers: Pathways to Healing* (Springer, 2009).

3 – 16. J R Smith, Series Editor, *Patient Pictures*, Health Press (14 books designed to explain procedures for patients – this series sold over 200,000 copies between 1995 and 2006).

17 – 21. Smith J R, Series Editor, *Guide to …* (Maxwell Publishing; 5 titles published 1991 – 1994).

For physicians:

22. J R Smith, G Del Priore, J Curtin, J Monaghan, *An Atlas of Gynaecological Surgery* (1st edition, Martin Dunitz, 2001).

23. J R Smith, G Del Priore, J Curtin, J Monaghan (2nd Edition, Taylor and Francis, 2007).

24. J R Smith, G Del Priore, R Coleman, J Monaghan (3rd Edition, Informa, 2012).

25. J R Smith, G Del Priore, R Coleman, J Monaghan (4th Edition 4, Informa, to be published 2016).

26. J R Smith, G Del Priore, J Healy, *An Atlas of Gynaecological Cancer Staging* (Springer, 2008).

27. J R Smith, B Baron, *Fast Facts: HIV in Obstetrics and Gynaecology* (Health Press, 1998).

28. J R Smith, B Baron, *Fast Facts: Gynaecological Oncology* (1st Edition, Health Press, 1998).

29. S Shahabi, J R Smith, G Del Priore, *Fast Facts: Gynaecological Oncology* (2nd Edition, 2012)

30. J R Smith, V S Kitchen, *Infection in Gynaecology* (Churchill Livingstone, 1993)

Foreword

Baroness Cox
Patron of Womb Transplant UK

It gives me great pleasure to write a foreword to this book as it is written for a very good cause: the enhancement of cancer survivorship.

As a double bonus it will also support the charity of which the author is chairman, and I am patron: Womb Transplant UK. With improving treatments over the last two to three decades, more and more women are surviving longer following their diagnosis of cancer; the majority can be assessed as 'cured'. However, one of the great difficulties for anyone who has had cancer is not knowing whether it will recur.

This book is designed to help people to live life to the full and to alleviate worry about the future. I believe that many will benefit from the 'tricks' described here, as well as enjoying the autobiographical nature of some of Richard Smith's stories.

I hope that you will derive pleasure and benefit from reading the book and I know that Womb Transplant UK will also benefit from your purchase!

The Baroness (Caroline) Cox of Queensbury

Preface

Richard Chartres

I Sometimes you could be forgiven, as you look at the Christian Church, for forgetting that it was Jesus Christ who told his followers that 'I am come that they might have life, and that they might have it more abundantly' (John's Gospel X.10). Here is a book about fullness of life, written by a man who certainly leads a very full life and whose spiritual life and professional life as a consultant gynaecologist are refreshingly seamless.

It is partly autobiographical, partly travelogue, and interwoven with insights from psychology, the wisdom of the saints, the blessings of pilgrimage, icons and music. It is edifying without being stuffy and Richard Smith is full of practical ideas and advice on how to live life to the full.

Baroness Cox has reminded us in her preface that the book will also raise money for a good cause and, like her, I hope that you will receive a blessing yourself as you also support the important work of the trust.

The Rt Revd & Rt Hon Richard Chartres KCVO DD FSA
Bishop of London

Introduction

As I write this book, the UK Uterine Transplant research team of surgeons, physicians and scientists which I have the honour and privilege to lead are close to starting a pioneering initiative to set up a sustainable programme of womb transplant operations – the first ever in Britain – for women either born without a womb or those who have had theirs surgically removed following treatment for cancer or other serious illness. I am very pleased to say that in 2015 we were granted ethics approval to perform a series of 10 transplants which, if successful, will lead to a sustainable national programme for womb transplantation. Our team hope to begin these operations within the next few months.

These two firsts are not unrelated. I have written a number of medical books before but never one with a spiritual theme, and I felt prompted to do so because of what I've learned from the privilege of working with the many women with cancer and amongst those who applied to be a part of the womb transplant procedure. Uterine transplantation and fertility sparing surgery for cancer, like this book, are all about *being whole*.

If asked what is the prime motivating factor of most of the women who wish to undergo this operation, a lot of people might say, well it's obvious: it's because they want to have a baby. But in my opinion, borne out by research conducted by the team, that's not quite right. In talking to these women (more than one hundred have been considered to be part of the initial trials) I've come to realise that many of the women who have lost, or are born without, their uterus feel that they have a gap in their lives, that they are somehow incomplete as women. I believe that what they want, more than anything else, is to feel like a *complete woman* with the potential to carry a baby inside them. This is also the motivation for many women to opt for slightly riskier fertility sparing surgery in the face of their cancer. The purpose of our research and the British womb transplant programme and the development of fertility sparing surgery has been to see its patients as whole people, and to be able to address their whole need – not just physical, but emotional and psychological, and some might say spiritual as well. I'm writing this book for precisely the same reason – it is about being *whole* in mind, body and spirit and understanding those other aspects of our personality.

At a more obvious, but no less important, level, this is a book about pilgrimage, long distance walking and the use of chant, all in pursuit of fitness and fulfillment. Happiness and contentment are very elusive things not dependent, in general, on money and material things, but rather on feelings of physical, mental and spiritual wellbeing – herein can wholeness be found.

To complete the book I have come to the Greek island of Patmos. This is the island where St John the Divine had his Revelation from God, dictated it to his scribe Prochorou who wrote it down and it subsequently became the last book of the New Testament. I have come here in pursuit of my own revelation, namely to turn a series of travelogues describing long distance walks, pilgrimages and other journeys into a coherent treatise with a relevant message and *modus operandi*. It will, I hope, reveal an ancient path to wholeness that many of you won't have considered before. In our materialistic world it's a path much denied and even vilified but the route is still there if one cares to look for it, or, even better, to take a few steps along the way – perhaps the first steps on a journey to some wonderful and life-changing new experiences.

My profession is a gynaecological cancer surgeon, and for

the last twenty years I have been a consultant. For the eleven years before that I was a junior doctor working around the West of Scotland and at St Mary's Hospital and the Westminster Hospital in London. In my time as a senior lecturer and consultant I have slowly moved round West London, from Charing Cross Hospital to Chelsea and Westminster Hospital and then to the West London Gynaecological Cancer Centre, Imperial College NHS Trust, based at Hammersmith and Charing Cross. When I left Charing Cross Hospital almost two decades ago I could not have imagined that I would be back in the same room ten years later. The décor, which was not good to start with, had hardly changed but one big thing which had changed over this period was a greatly enhanced cure rate for patients diagnosed with cancer. Even for those not cured there is now a far greater prospect of living for much longer periods of time with good quality of life between bouts of unpleasant, but mercifully short-term, treatment. The cancers I treat arise in the uterus (womb), cervix (neck of the womb), vagina, vulva (the skin on the outside of the vagina), the ovaries, Fallopian tubes and finally gestational trophoblastic disease (cancers of the afterbirth).

Cancer of the uterus usually causes vaginal bleeding, either between periods or after the menopause, and women tend to go early to their doctor meaning that diagnosis can occur fast and there is a far greater chance of treatment that is successful in terms of cure and onward quality of life. Over the last thirty years treatment and cure rates have remained similar but times of recovery from surgery have improved greatly thanks to a combination of improved techniques and better recovery procedures. The very successful smear program has hugely increased the diagnosis of and cure rate for women with cervical cancer, often with fertility being spared.

Over the past forty years or so huge changes have taken place in the challenges facing patients with ovarian cancer.

When I was a medical student in the 1970s the average survival time for a woman with ovarian cancer, including all stages, was ten months after diagnosis. Staging of cancers refers to where in the body the cancer has spread to: Stage I, meaning confined to the ovaries, has always carried a high (>90%) cure rate; for Stages III and IV, meaning that the cancer has spread in the abdomen or chest, the best treatment centres are now reporting more than 50% of their patients achieving at least five years of survival. Sadly most of these women will not be cured, but by five years after their diagnosis they will probably have been treated once at the start with surgery and chemotherapy, and then retreated one or more times with chemotherapy and perhaps also with surgery again.

One of the great difficulties for all cancer patients and their families is that they never know whether they are on the good side or the bad side of the ever-improving statistics. It has been my observation over many years that some patients will roll with their diagnosis and its uncertainties, ironically discovering that their cancer diagnosis makes them value every day they have far more than they were doing before the diagnosis; many of those who survive long term will say that the cancer was the thing that made them live their lives better and appreciate it more. For patients who have a disease with a lower cure rate but a higher chance of many years of survival, the psychological challenge is yet greater, but many people rise to this challenge and really live it. Everybody – the patients themselves, their families, doctors and nurses – would love to be able to 'give it the all clear', but sadly this is not the reality of the disease, at least not until several years have passed by. In gynaecology we are luckier than some specialities because, for most of our patients, if they remain disease-free for five years then they really are 'in the clear'. Sometimes cancers do come back later but this is very unlikely. In fact, for most of our patients after five years there is more chance of them developing a new, completely unrelated cancer than having a recurrence of the original one.

Those presenting with advanced ovarian cancer are much less likely than those with the other cancers to go for five years without recurrence, which makes it much harder to maintain positivity. Sadly some breast cancer patients, depending upon the type, also have to live with the uncertainty for long periods of time, which is very hard. One of my previous books, *Women's Cancers: Pathways to Healing*, and its updated successor, *Women's Cancers: Pathways to Living*, address many of these issues in more detail.

As well as those patients who are able to cope well, even flourish, there are many I work with who do really struggle and feel weighed down by their own potential mortality. It is one of life's great ironies: we all know that our own death is 100% inevitable, but we go through our lives believing in our own immortality. The cancer diagnosis – like other conditions such as heart attacks, diabetes and high blood pressure – always shakes the 'immortality belief' to its core. The other conditions do tend to be considered a bit differently from cancer, though. I regularly sit in my clinic discussing the mortality figures for a 70-year-old with a breast cancer diagnosis (40% of breast cancer diagnoses occur at the age of 70 or higher) compared to those for a 70-year-old diagnosed with a fractured hip: the woman with breast cancer has a 70% chance of being alive five years later, while the woman with the fracture has a 50% chance of dying within the next five years, and a 50% chance that she will never walk unaided again.

I am writing this book partly in response to reflections I have had in the course of caring for my patients, and the search for strategies to cope with challenging emotions. But it has also arisen from difficulties that I have faced myself, both physical and personal, so now it's time for me to tell you a little bit of my own story.

The Journey

Some years ago, when my first two children Cameron and Victoria were still young, I contrived to get a divorce from my ex-wife Val, as one might expect, a highly traumatic time for all concerned. Soon thereafter I developed a chest pain which prompted a trip to the cardiologist, where mercifully I was diagnosed only with reflux oesophagitis and Helicobacter. However, within three weeks I developed acute peritonitis on the back of a strangulated gangrenous hernia. At that time I was on the waiting list for a bilateral hernia repair. On the day of my diagnosis I told my new partner Deborah (now my wife) that I thought my hernia might be strangulating. She told me 'not to be so daft', so I duly went off to my clinic where, as the morning progressed, my abdominal pain increased to the point that I could no longer stand up straight. I looked like one of those caricatures of an old man with lumbago.

I phoned Deborah to tell her that I was going to the physiotherapists' gym to hang upside down. She told me again not to be daft, but this time to go and see a surgeon. I tottered round to the clinic next door to my own, where Meirion Thomas, a famous cancer surgeon, was consulting. He told me to get on to his couch, where he felt my belly and immediately told me that I had acute peritonitis and needed a laparotomy (in other words, I needed to be opened up!). I asked him when and he said: 'Now!' 'But I've just eaten a sandwich!' I protested, to which he declared me a stupid **** and said that he would operate on me at five o'clock that afternoon.

Before my operation I went back to my own theatre and performed a small procedure, which I knew I could do sitting down (I was only in pain when standing upright). I knew that the patient who was on that afternoon would have a big delay over starting radiotherapy if I failed to do the necessary that day. I then got in my car, drove to the Lister Hospital about two miles away, clambered into the hospital bed and at five was taken to theatre where Meirion sorted me out.

The following day was highly instructive for me on a number of levels. After twenty years working in hospitals I had never realised that, as a patient, the quality of one's individual experience at any point in time is entirely down to the nurse looking after you. Which doctor you get is largely irrelevant! In the twenty-four hours that I was in, I had one nurse who was awful, one who was average and one who was excellent. By the time I returned to work four weeks later, one of the patients I had operated on the day before my own crisis had made an official complaint about the awful nurse and she had been dismissed for this and a number of other uncaring incidents.

The day after my operation I was told that I still didn't look too well. Various doctors appeared, and the suggestion was made that I had either had a myocardial infarction (a heart attack) and needed to be transferred to the Royal Brompton Hospital for an angiogram, or that I had had a pulmonary embolism (a blood clot on the lung). I took great delight in declaring that I had had my normal angiogram three weeks earlier, so a heart attack was off the agenda. But in response to the suggestion of blood clots on the lung I was less sanguine. In fact, I behaved very badly indeed. I told the nurses that I was not prepared to have the necessary CT scan of my lungs to check for clots. In my defence, I was in the midst of trying to get a mortgage at this time and was also full of morphine after the operation so I think my senses weren't at their sharpest.

The Resident Medical Officer was called. The poor fellow had recently been one of my juniors, so it was a tricky situation for him. I told him I did not want investigated at all because it might ruin my mortgage application, and then told him in no uncertain terms that I was really f***ed off with the whole business and – just to make sure he really understood my frustrations – I wrenched the IV cannula drip out of my arm and threw it across the room. The doctor looked at me and said, very gently: 'I can see you are very upset, Mr Smith.' Ten minutes later this very fine young man had persuaded me to have my cannula re-sited and I was in a wheelchair heading for my CT scan, meek as a lamb. I'm delighted to say that Arvind Vashisht is now a senior doctor in an august institution, doing very good work very well and deservedly.

Just to absolutely drive home to me the gravity of my situation, I was wheeled past my friend and colleague, plastic surgeon Adam Searle, who looked visibly shocked on seeing me. Even through the morphine I could see this. He commented that I looked terrible. Happy luck, the CT showed no clots, just a slight pneumonia, so I was put on to antibiotics and the following day I took my own discharge, with Meirion's tacit approval. He said I was making people nervous. The whole experience had been quite the wake-up call for me. My own sense of personal invincibility had been completely challenged and mortality became a reality to me.

Post-divorce and remarriage, my life settled into a routine of seeing my children on alternate weekends and holidays. This adjustment was hard, and I had an underlying fear that my ex-wife might take my children to the USA. This became such a concern for me that I returned to see Suzanne Thomas, the counsellor and hypnotherapist of whom I had been a client during the divorce. After just an hour she declared me non-paranoid but perhaps prescient, and told me that I did not need counseling. Sure enough, three days later my ex-wife announced that she had landed a great job in Philadelphia and so she and the children did indeed move abroad. My ex-wife is a very clever woman, ultimately becoming senior vice-president of a major pharmaceutical company, and she deserves all the success she has achieved. However, this move, the legal ramifications and the children's departure caused great sadness for me.

Out of most bad things comes some good, for British

Introduction

Airways as well as for me as I took to travelling to the USA two or three times a year, to see the children and managing to do some business while I was there. My great friend Giuseppe Del Priore and I co-edited multiple books during my times in the States. Our editorial meetings usually took place in the Woodrow Wilson service area on the New Jersey Turnpike, about half-way between Philadelphia and New York, which allowed us to work together for many hours at a time, get breakfast and for me to get back on time to collect the kids from school. This was only for two or three short periods of time a year, but way better than never. Just in case you are thinking the Woodrow Wilson sounds cool, it's not. I am afraid the food is very bad for one, although reasonably tasty. I used to turn up in my hire car, usually a Chrysler Sebring convertible or a Mustang, which might all sound very smooth and expensive but I promise you it is not. A convertible car out of Glasgow Airport would be £450 for two days, while in Philadelphia £150 does the trick for three or four days, the gasoline is cheap and driving around with the roof down made the children – and me – very happy!

I was always casually dressed in jeans, t-shirt and fleece, while Giuseppe would usually turn up in his Porsche 911 convertible, dressed in his Armani suit and looking every inch the Manhattan Professor of Gynaecology, which he was. He looked as if he had stepped in from a different planet, which in many ways, to me, he had. Giuseppe is a very special man, whom it has been a great privilege to count as a friend. He and I used to get through an enormous power of work between school hours, ultimately notching up eight books and a shared research program which produced many more publications. The children also came to stay with me in the UK for New Year, summer and Easter holidays, and as they grew older it became easier for me to rationalise this.

The juxtaposition of personal ill health with personal, family and social disaster was a seriously mind-focusing experience. Although I did not realise it at the time, I was undergoing a grief response to my situations. This response has been codified by American physician Elisabeth Kübler-Ross, in her brilliant book *On Death and Dying*, as DABDA: Denial; Anger; Bewilderment/Bargaining; Depression; Acceptance. These emotions in truth can occur in any order and they certainly did in me. They are the same response someone can get when given a cancer diagnosis, either for oneself or for one's nearest and dearest.

I had run a hypnotherapy clinic for many years and at that time of my life was regularly self-hypnotising to some effect as just one means of coping, while also having hypnotherapy and counseling from Suzanne Thomas. After a year, Suzanne told me that there was nothing more she could do for me and suggested that I was actually seeking some sort of absolution for my sins – not something that she nor anybody else was able to give me. She did however suggest that I go to see the Reverend Gary Bradley, the vicar of Little Venice, the parish in which I lived, as I had mentioned his name to her a few times. Fr Gary had baptised Cameron and Victoria, and I had taken him for dinner afterwards to say thank you.

I was not a regular churchgoer; I had been brought up in the Church of Scotland, but had let that all go by the time I was a teenager. Religion was not something that fitted into my somewhat sybaritic student and junior doctor life. My ex-brother-in-law Paul Reid even previously commented that with my past I needed a good dose of religion to have any chance in the next life! But when the children were baptised I felt very drawn to the Anglo-Catholic mass that was part of the service. This style of worship is almost indistinguishable from the Roman Catholic liturgy, except that it is even higher church, with Greek and Latin used during parts of the ceremony.

Following Suzanne's suggestion I arranged to meet Gary at his home. I arrived at seven and Gary opened a bottle of red wine and asked me how I was. He did not get a quick reply! He did, however, ask me some questions, relating to my marriage vows.

For richer for poorer, where was I now? Poorer, but still paying my dues, I replied. In sickness and in health, where was I now? Plenty of sickness, I replied.

Of course I had failed many of my vows, but I felt a little better for talking about this with Gary. He went on to tell me that another cleric had told him that he thought the marriage vows were like a fine porcelain vase: very beautiful while the vase is intact, but woe betide you if you break that vase. You can put it back together again, but it will never have the same beauty. This seemed to me to be a pretty fair summary of where I was at.

Thereafter, I started going to Gary's Sunday service on a regular basis. Deborah started to come too. Gary took me through confirmation classes and when Deborah and I got married (in a registry office), he gave us a wonderful service of blessing. He subsequently baptised our two little children Madeleine and Lara, who are both now happily ensconced in the Church of England education system.

Suzanne has my eternal gratitude for pushing me in Gary's direction but also for one further introduction, namely to the works of the late Laurens Van Der Post and in particular his book *Jung and the Story of Our Time*, his biography of the great Swiss psychologist Carl Gustav Jung. This particular book led me to read most of everything else that both these men wrote. They are both rather unfashionable in modern psychology, but for me they, and Gary, opened up a whole new world of which I had previously known nothing.

I was about to embark on a Journey, and part of that Journey has been a series of smaller journeys, some of which I am going to tell you about in this book.

JERUSALEM
The Holy City

Day 1

The American Colony Hotel is a very beautiful building, the artistic design of which shows a heavy Islamic influence. My wife Deborah and I awoke to the scent of trees and herbs from the garden through the open window of our bedroom suite. We and our two travelling companions – Robert Chandler and Fr Gary Bradley – had arrived, exhausted, in Jerusalem the night before following a fifty-minute drive from the airport in Tel Aviv and another hour spent trying to find our hotel. Jerusalem is an extremely confusing place for newcomers to drive around in the dark and we took a slight 'Bonfire of the Vanities' wrong turn, ending up going down a very long winding hill, through some fairly poor markets which seemed to get poorer the lower down the hill we went, and ended up in a part of Jerusalem that we really shouldn't have been in. After a rapid three-point turn, we made it back up the hill and eventually, with the help of a few Israelis along the way, found our hotel.

After breakfast we walked into the city and the very first church that we walked past was St George's, the Anglican cathedral in Jerusalem. This was an unplanned, happy chance and it seemed extremely appropriate for this little group of four Anglo-Catholic pilgrims. St. George's Cathedral is just like an English parish church so one couldn't help but feel immediately at home. Abutting it was the Anglican guesthouse and various memorials to the British Mandate for Palestine, including the Royal Coat of Arms which used to hang in Government House during the Mandate years of 1922 to 1948. The church itself has a classic, Victorian gothic-style tower, undoubtedly 'a corner of Jerusalem which is forever England', to paraphrase Rupert Brooke.

From there, we walked down through the Arabic market and Herod's Gate, then zig-zagged through the old city until we found the Via Dolorosa. There, we were grabbed by a shop owner who insisted on taking us to see the first two Stations of the Cross. The first is a beautiful church built in the nineteenth century, I think by the Franciscans, with a crown of thorns in its dome. Immediately opposite is the second church, built by the Franciscans in about 1900 and also very beautiful. We were then taken to the convent containing the Ecce Homo ('Behold the Man') church, and from there down thirty feet to the lower ground level where the original Roman road and cisterns are visible. To the accompaniment of some rather haunting singing from a couple of small parties of Orthodox pilgrims we found the slab where it is reputed the soldiers cast dice for Christ's clothes, and then a part of the actual road on which Christ would have trod, carrying his cross on the way to his crucifixion.

> *These stones that have echoed their praises are holy, and dear is the ground where their feet have once trod; yet here they confessed they were strangers and pilgrims, and still they were seeking the city of god.*
>
> *Sing praise, then, for all who here fought and here found him, whose journey is ended, whose perils are past: they believed in the light; and its glory is round them, where the clouds of earth's sorrow are lifted at last.*
>
> *William H Draper 'In Our Day of Thanksgiving'.*

There was little to mark this place out as a religious site yet there was a heavy spiritual atmosphere. I felt compelled to kiss the ground, after which Gary pointed out the stones would have been slippery with excrement at the time Christ was painfully shouldering his cross to walk up this particular street.

We emerged into the daylight and had to satisfy our guide by purchasing something in his shop. Gary managed a knockdown rate for twelve rosaries. Deborah bought three silver crucifixes and we thanked the man for his guidance and headed off due West up the Via Dolorosa in the direction of the Christian quarter.

We took a small detour up to the Damascus Gate and from there rejoined the Via Dolorosa at a point closer to the Church of the Holy Sepulchre, stopping at the various Stations along the way. Hundreds of shops line these streets, all mixed together in one vast souk, selling all manner of things from antiques, religious tat and ancient artefacts to pornographic movies, CDs and cheap clothes. We approached the Russian Twelfth Station of the Cross where Jesus exited the Gate of the City (not recognised as such by Catholics), and we passed through the Eye of the Needle, a hole in the wall next to the main gate through which a camel couldn't pass. We all managed to pass through the Eye, although we could think of a few friends who couldn't! This station has two very beautiful chapels and a large protruding rock which would have been there are the time of Christ on his route to Golgotha. In the Alexander Nevsky chapel we discovered a number of icons, relics of St Haralambos and St Panteleimon amongst others. Haralambos is the patron saint of the Ionian and at home I have an eighteenth-century icon of him perched on the hill above one of my favourite monasteries at Kathara in Ithaca, Greece. Panteleimon is the Russian patron saint of doctors and I also have an antique Victorian icon of him so much of what we saw here resonated with me.

Thereafter we entered the courtyard of the Church of the Holy Sepulchre where there were a huge number of people milling around, and into the church itself, which was absolutely packed at the main sites. As we walked through the first vestibule the sun was shining through the dome above our heads, combining with the carillon bells being played to enhance what was already a very beautiful site. Near the entrance was a large stone slab by which a lot of people were kneeling and crying, kissing the stone and placing prayers on it, suggesting that it was an object of great significance, though we knew not what.

To our left was the site where Christ's tomb is thought to have been but unfortunately there was a huge queue, and it would probably have taken at least an hour if not longer, to enter the small chapel. Effectively this is an orthodox church within the church and we decided against queuing, going instead to the small Coptic church at the very back of the shrine, and in fact in there is a slab on which the Coptics have written 'here Jesus Christ was buried'. This is probably about a foot and a half away from the slab on the other side which everybody was queuing for. I paid my 20 shekels for a candle and was allowed to kneel and kiss this stone. Interestingly when we returned later this area was roped off, so I had been in luck!

We passed various other chapels within the church, none of which we could get into because there were too many people. We went upstairs and were fortunate that we appeared to have got ahead of the crowd and were able to queue to get into the chapel at Golgotha where the cross is thought to have been implanted into the rocks. As we walked up the steep staircase to effectively twenty to thirty feet above the ground floor of the church, I wondered why the shrine to the crucifixion was so far up above ground level. The answer of course is that the crag on which the church has been placed must have been about thirty to forty feet high to allow any crucified men to be seen across the whole of Jerusalem. Above the actual place of crucifixion is an altar table and above this an enormous orthodox image of Christ on the cross set in a silver oklad surrounded by tens of lampadas. A priest was there, standing on a ladder to fill the lampadas with oil. Under the altar table is a brass circular plate with a hole in the middle. I watched Gary go forward first; he crossed himself, kissed the plate and put his hand into the hole in the plate, allowing him to touch the rock where the cross once sat. Then it was Robert's turn, then Deborah's, then my own.

I had been deputed to place the bag with all of the day's memorabilia shopping in it (including twelve rosaries, a number of crucifixes and other bits and bobs such as a tub of saffron) on to the brass plate, for the blessing of Calvary. I also pulled out my own crucifix, a nineteenth-century Coptic cross on a leather necklace, but somewhat disturbingly the necklace disintegrated in my hands as I gently removed it from my shirt. I then put my hand into the hole, undoubtedly a very moving experience. The rock below is smooth with the touching of millions of pilgrims over something in the region of sixteen hundred years. My wooden Chotki was in my hand and so can also claim the distinction of having touched the rock. The saffron would be used at a later date to make a 'holy paella' – a must for Gary and Robert coming round for dinner. We then made a contribution, bought candles and emerged out onto the balcony in the upper part of the church. There was a very heavy air of genuine religiousness permeating this place, despite the huge numbers of people thronging through its doors.

We started to go back down the stairs but discovered the staircase was blocked. I thought initially that it was probably a bunch of youths who were being lazy and having a rest, but we realised that there was a big procession about to enter the church, causing people to be shepherded back. The sound of the bells should have warned me something was about to happen! The four of us ran back up the steps to get a good view, and to do so I found myself having to hang like a monkey off a light fitting, standing on the edge of a balcony where one step back would have resulted in a twenty-foot drop. From here though we were able to see four individuals wearing fezzes and each thumping on the floor a large black rod with a heavy steel-weighted base, making a deafening noise. A large processional choir entered and started to sing. More people entered, including a large number of clergy among whom was the Archbishop or Metropolitan or some such who was double-cloaked at the door of the church. There was another wonderful ringing of the carillon bells.

I was unable to take any photos since I had no hands free to stop me from falling. When the procession had moved on and we finally made it back downstairs, the crowds had begun to clear and we were able to go into each of the little chapels. We came across a section of glassed-in stonework that was directly beneath the position of the cross from which we had just descended. This is part of the crag that makes up the site of Golgotha. I now have a very clear view in my head as to what this site must have looked like at the time of the crucifixion, and it is very different view from what I previously had envisaged. This was not 'a green hill far away'.

On our way out we passed once again the slab whose significance we hadn't known. I took off my crucifix and popped it on the stone, kissed the stone along with many tens of other pilgrims doing likewise. I assumed that the stone was a segment of the path that Christ must have trodden when climbing the hill to Golgotha. In fact, as we discovered later, it was the stone of anointing of Christ after his death when he was taken down from the cross.

Finally, we emerged somewhat stunned into the daylight and immediately repaired to more religious iconography shops where we purchased some gifts for ourselves and various friends. On our way back to the hotel we spotted a sign for 'the garden tomb'. Gary and I had previously agreed that we probably wouldn't visit this site – a tomb (in which it is claimed Jesus' body was laid) in an area of cliff face which has a slight appearance of a skull and therefore thought to be Golgotha – but as it was there, in we went.

The site itself – with various groups of people holding services and singing hymns between the cypress trees – is beautiful, although the view of the skull-like cliff face has been marred by some town-planner inserting a bus station beneath it. To be honest, I didn't find it as spiritually uplifting as the Church of the Holy Sepulchre but there were plenty of people there who appeared to be emotionally-moved by the site and that, at the end of the day, is what matters. To my mind it seems inconceivable that the church of the Holy Sepulchre had been planted in the wrong place and thus I struggled to believe that Jesus himself was ever placed in this particular tomb in this particular garden. Gary suggested that the Victorian British who established this site didn't want to be tied in with the Coptics, Armenians, Orthodox and Roman Catholics also present in the city and so decided to set up something of their own just outside the medieval city walls. All the world's Christian denominations have tried to have a little share of Jerusalem: the Scots and the English originally came with the Crusaders, but the Victorians, who already ruled a quarter of the globe, most likely wanted a bigger part of Jerusalem and so settled on the idea of this garden tomb.

There are so many historical layers to this city: the original Roman layer which is pretty well hidden for the most part, then the medieval layer which comprises most of what there is to see in the Old City. On top of that is the Victorian layer – the period in which all the great powers of that time built their monuments. The Russians built the Church of St Mary Magdalene on the slopes of the Mount of Olives, the English built St George's Cathedral, the Scots built St Andrew's Hospice and General Gordon of Kharthoum founded this garden tomb. The French built on the Mount of

Olives, and the Germans built the huge Lutheran church on the Via Dolorosa.

The big question for me is not who built them and when, but why these places resonate so. I believe it is that the reality of the Christian story becomes so much more when one stands at the sites at which events took place – either actually or in the close vicinity. The twenty-first century 'take' that most of what is written in the New Testament is some form of fairytale just falls away. One also gains new perspectives – most of us have read the Bible stories, but I for one had not realized how physically close together all these sites were and are – which in themselves give additional credibility.

The Celtic view would be that this is a 'thin place', in other words a place where one senses God very strongly. Jerusalem has to be the thinnest place I have been – and I consider it even more remarkable that such thinness is found in the middle of a bustling city. Most of the other thin places I have experienced are in the remote countryside, such as on Iona, Bute and Mount Athos, but Jerusalem's Old City is essentially shops and commercialism. Maybe that seems okay here because of its Roman and medieval feel, which helps one better imagine what it must have been like in the time of Christ. Whatever the explanations, this is a very powerful spiritual place – no more than one might expect to find in the centre of Christianity, Judaism and Islam.

Later in the day – after a return to our hotel for refreshments – we hailed a taxi and visited the two likely sites of Emmaus, on the road to which the resurrected Jesus was seen by his disciples Cleopas and Simon. It seemed appropriate to make this trip on the same day that we had been to the site of Christ's death and burial. There has been a lot of argument about the true site of Emmaus – we in fact decided to cover two of the three options. We went first to what is probably the archaeologically-true site, Al Mosa, although there is actually nothing to see there apart from an old fort. Then we went on to Abu Gosh, the traditional site of Emmaus and probably too far away to be the real one, but where there is a very beautiful crusader church. The third site is now a Franciscan monastery and is too far away from Jerusalem to be the real site; it would have been impossible for Cleopas and Simon to walk back to Jerusalem by nightfall having seen Jesus, even if they were Olympic athletes!

Gary had visited the Abu Gosh church fifteen years previously when it was part of a village in the countryside. Now it is in the middle of a large housing estate and more a part of Jerusalem. This does not, however, detract from the beauty of the church in its wonderful gardens once you have stepped through the surrounding walls. There were many other pilgrims there and we could hear singing from inside the church. Gary read the story of Cleopas and Simon from my copy of the New Testament:

And, behold, two of them went that same day to a village called Emmaus, which was from Jerusalem about threescore furlongs.

And they talked together of all these things which had happened.

And it came to pass, that, while they communed together and reasoned, Jesus himself drew near, and went with them.

But their eyes were holden that they should not know him.

And he said unto them, What manner of communications are these that ye have one to another, as ye walk, and are sad?

And the one of them, whose name was Cleopas, answering said unto him, Art thou only a stranger in Jerusalem, and hast not known the things which are come to pass there in these days?

And he said unto them, What things? And they said unto him, Concerning Jesus of Nazareth, which was a prophet mighty in deed and word before God and all the people:

And how the chief priests and our rulers delivered him to be condemned to death, and have crucified him.

But we trusted that it had been he which should have redeemed Israel: and beside all this, today is the third day since these things were done.

Yea, and certain women also of our company made us astonished, which were early at the sepulchre;

And when they found not his body, they came, saying, that they had also seen a vision of angels, which said that he was alive.

And certain of them which were with us went to the sepulchre, and found it even so as the women had said: but him they saw not.

Then he said unto them, O fools, and slow of heart to believe all that the prophets have spoken:

Ought not Christ to have suffered these things, and to enter into his glory?

And beginning at Moses and all the prophets, he expounded unto them in all the scriptures the things concerning himself.

And they drew nigh unto the village, whither they went: and he made as though he would have gone further.

But they constrained him, saying, Abide with us: for it is towards evening, and the day is far spent. And he went in to tarry with them.

And it came to pass, as he sat at meat with them, he took bread, and blessed it, and brake, and gave to them.

And their eyes were opened, and they knew him; and he vanished out of their sight.

And they said one to another, Did not our heart burn

within us, while he talked with us by the way, and while he opened to us the scriptures?

And they rose up the same hour, and returned to Jerusalem, and found the eleven gathered together, and them that were with them,

Saying, The Lord is risen indeed, and hath appeared to Simon.

And they told what things were done in the way and how he was known of them in breaking of bread.

And as they thus spake, Jesus himself stood in the midst of them, and saith unto them, Peace be unto you.

(Luke 24: 13-36)

This was a fitting end to our first day's pilgrimage in Jerusalem – a truly remarkable day. I had wanted very much to do this trip and often, when one wants very much to do something, it comes as a slight disappointment when you actually do it. But not this time. The day exceeded all my expectations. All the religious tat and the nasty shops (nor the good shops!) could not detract from the fact that Jerusalem is an amazing place.

There is no doubting that what we experienced today was something of enormous and vital importance. The tragedy of Dawkins and his atheistic zealotry is that he is no different from any other religious zealot. I believe that those who pit religion against science and suggest that the two viewpoints are incompatible are totally wrong. It is entirely compatible to be a scientist and to hold deep religious conviction. I have spent a lifetime steeped in science and medicine. Mathematics was my best subject at school and at that time I understood Einstein's Theory of Relativity and the elegance of it. Yet this does not detract in any way from the mystical experience I discovered this day in the Holy City.

ðay 2

I was awoken this morning by Deborah attempting to leave quietly for a swim in the hotel pool, and after a quarter of an hour I decided to join her. The pool was outdoors and the water was not nearly as welcoming as it had seemed last night after a bottle of claret and a generous helping of Laphroaig. At that juncture I had popped a finger into the pool and thought that it felt of bath-like warmth. The morning swim promptly disabused me of this illusion. It was, however, refreshing and was followed by a hearty breakfast with Gary and Robert, at which we decided that if we wanted to fit in everything we wanted to see on our second day in Jerusalem then we would do better to take a cab than to set out on foot again.

By happy chance Moza, the driver who had taken us to Emmaus, happened to be at the head of the queue in the hotel taxi rank. Moza drove us to the top of the Mount of Olives, from where we looked out over the whole city and managed to identify Mount Zion, the more obvious features of the Dome of the Rock, the King David Hotel, St George's Cathedral, the Church of the Holy Sepulchre, the grave stones of the Kidron Valley and the Garden of Gethsemane at its base. However many books one reads and pictures one sees, it is not possible to get a place into perspective until one has seen it in the flesh. Jerusalem from this viewpoint is truly one of the amazing sights of the world, a bit like the first time one sees the Acropolis or the ancient parts of Rome. It did remind me of both although of course it is a lot older than Ancient Rome and also much more fought over.

The last time Gary had been here there were no observation points on top of the Mount, nor roads down through the stone-piled graves, like the one we descended now. I thought at first that the graves were just untidy but Deborah explained to me that there is a Jewish tradition for people who have been at a burial to return each year and place a rock upon the grave.

The first church at which we stopped on our descent was the Dominus Flavit Chapel. This is a modern Franciscan construction, shaped like a teardrop since it was here that Christ cried for the fate of Jerusalem. The view from the window, which we unfortunately couldn't get to because there was a private mass going on inside, is the famous shot used in so many books where one is looking through glass with a crucifix in the foreground and the dome of the rock in the background.

From here we continued down the hill to the Garden of Gethsemane, which had also changed since Gary's last visit, less accessible now but still beautiful, full of old olive trees which were – if not the actual olive trees that Christ sat under – perhaps grown from their cuttings. This is the garden in which Jesus prayed while his disciples fell asleep, where Judas betrayed him and Peter cut off the Roman guard's ear.

We entered Gethsemane's Church of All Nations, a Roman Catholic Church which has bare rock under the altar where Christ prayed and sweated blood. This area was walled off but about ten minutes into our wandering round, admiring the various mosaics, an American congregation entered the church and were ushered into its centre, around the altar. We sat on a pew outside and were able to partake in a delightful service presided over by an Irish-American from Wisconsin for his parishioners, two of whom turned out to be doctors. The group's leader, a kind Christian Palestinian, saw that we had joined in the service, unlocked the gate to the altar and invited us in to join them for communion. This gave us an opportunity to get close to the rock and to kiss it. Before this trip I had never kissed a rock in my life, but it was beginning to become a habit!

Following the service we walked across the road to the Tomb of the Dormition of the Virgin, which is the site where the Virgin was buried and from where she ascended, according to tradition. This Russian Orthodox shrine is deep underground, and small so we had to bow low to get into it and then queue to venerate the icon. A group of Franciscans were holding a church service in the Catholic grotto next to it.

Moza was waiting outside as he had promised and when we had finished exploring Gethsemane he whisked us further down the Kidron Valley and up to the entrance to the old city at the Western Wall, otherwise known as the Wailing Wall, the most important Judaic religious site. What appeared to be tight security was in fact no such thing, since our bags were not searched or even x-rayed as we entered the Old City. Gary, Robert and I donned skull cups and headed for the male part of the Wall, while Deborah, who had a pashmina which doubled-up as a scarf, went to the female part. The Western Wall is the only surviving part of the second temple which was around at the time of Jesus and was mostly destroyed by the Romans in AD70. The Jewish belief is that at some point in the future the temple will be rebuilt. All the cracks in the wall are stuffed with paper where people's prayers have been placed, and here the physical presence of God is often remembered with the words of Deuteronomy 6: 4-7:

'Hear O Israel the Lord your God is one lord; and you shall love the Lord your God with all your heart, and with your soul, and with all your might. And these words that I

*command you this day shall be upon your heart and you
shall teach them diligently to your children and shall talk
to them when you sit in your house, and when you walk by
the way and when you lie down and when you rise'.*

We could hear a loud wailing noise coming from the female
section and when Robert and I asked what it was, Gary said
'It's Deborah ululating.' I must admit I thought at first that he
had said 'It's Deborah ovulating' – usually a silent process.

We left the Jewish sector of the Old City and turned right
into the Muslim sector, hoping to go straight to the Dome of
the Rock. In fact we got waylaid by a falafel lunch, served by
a man with the dirtiest fingernails I have ever seen in my life.
While everybody else tucked heartily into their salads, I stuck
with the falafel dipped in tahini and was still praying, as I
wrote this journal at the end of the trip, that I was not going to
suffer ill-effects from it! I decided that more Laphraoig might
be a wise precaution to stave off this possibility.

Having satisfactorily fed most of us, our café owner
directed us back down past the Western Wall to gain access to
the Dome of the Rock. We had to go through further security
and up a long ramp to a section of the Old City in which there
are two huge, golden onion-domed mosques, one of which is
the Dome of the Rock which houses the Stone of Abraham –
the foundation of both Judaism and of its offspring, namely
Christianity and Islam. To our tremendous disappointment,
we were not allowed in. The once welcoming entrance area
which used to be for the washing of hands and removal of
shoes had been closed and boards were placed round it,
denying even its architecture to external view, and the security
man on the door very rudely told us that we could not go in
because we were non-Muslim.

Can you imagine the outcry if there was a sign up at
Westminster Abbey or St Paul's Cathedral which said 'No

Muslims', and somebody on the door enforcing it? I have never been into a mosque in my life and have always been curious to see inside one. But we had to be content with taking a nice photograph of the Russian Orthodox Cathedral, of which we had a great view on the Mount of Olives opposite, before heading back through the Muslim quarter to our waiting taxi which returned us to the hotel.

To keep the pace rolling and to avoid being out on the road after nightfall we had a quick change of clothes then jumped into our hire car and motored out of Jerusalem to find, after a few wrong turns, the Jericho road. With a bit of foresight we might have thought better of entering the West Bank area in an Israeli-plated car! We had no intention of going into any of the towns, however, and we drove past Ramallah and then down on to Jericho. It is a remarkable part of the world, in the desert and surrounded by high mountains yet all well below sea level. The Dead Sea, as far as I know, is the lowest place on land on Earth, and the city of Jericho which we skirted is one of the oldest cities on Earth, people having lived there since 10,000 BC. Our plan had been to go to Qumran, have a swim – or, should I say, float – in the Dead Sea, and visit Masada – all hopelessly optimistic.

We arrived at Qumran and saw the site of the Essenes and the caves where the Dead Sea Scrolls were found. It is thought that Jesus probably lived in this community from the age of 12 up until he came into his ministry aged 30. The caves themselves – high in the crumbling limestone cliffs – looked extremely dangerous to get to and we speculated as to how the Bedouin shepherd boy who had found the scrolls there in the 1940s had found his way in. There is a high chance one would break one's neck trying that particular stunt. We could only imagine that maybe one of his goats had fallen into one of the caves and he was trying to get it back out.

We started to travel further down the shoreline – which was somewhat marred by huge quantities of barbed wire – passed by some palm tree plantations, and caught sight of the odd camel. Before too long we came to a roadblock with a high security tower from which a man with a machine gun kept watch across the Dead Sea towards Jordan. We decided at that point that we had gone far enough and that we weren't going to have time to swim in the inland sea, nor reach Masada, so headed back to Jerusalem.

day 3

Today, Moza took us out of Jerusalem, through the Palestinian territories and on to Bethlehem. The stark contrast to what we had experienced so far as we entered the Palestinian territories could not have been stronger. There were virtually no cars, and those few that we did see were beaten up and old. The whole place looked poverty-stricken and I felt quite a threatening air as we drove up through the hills to Bethlehem. We passed sheep grazing on the hillside but there the similarities to the Bethlehem we think of as the place of Jesus' birth end. There are now 170,000 people living in the town, and more than one hundred buses carrying around 5000 additional visitors turn up every day.

Our first port of call was the medieval crusader church in Manger Square, with the Gate of Humility at one end and a mosque at the other. It looked relatively quiet when we arrived but by the time Deborah had popped into the Italian hotel attached to the Franciscan monastery for a comfort stop, the crowds had amassed. There was some delay before we reached the head of the queue, where a Palestinian policeman asked us which party we were in. We declared that we were in our own party and he asked us how we had got there. We told him 'by taxi' from Jerusalem. He instantly informed us that, instead of queuing to go through the Gate of Humility with its ancient low lintel, we could, if we wished, move to the left and enter the church by a different route. Regardless, we chose the Gate, not realising that on the other side, once one had gone through the narthex of the church, there was a vast two-hour long queue to get to the chapel where Christ's birthplace and manger were.

The church itself was full of scaffolding with very little available to see. Its frescos were mostly faded away. There was some old excavation from the time of Justinian on display but before we had an opportunity to see anything we were approached by a Palestinian tour guide who offered to show us all the sights for the princely price of 100 shekels. We didn't feel particularly comfortable with this but with our taxi waiting to take us away in half an hour we suspected that our entire trip would have been in vain if we didn't follow him. He then proceeded, in a fairly irreligious fashion, to explain the church to us. It rapidly became clear that, having identified us as potentially 'rich' because we had come by taxi from Jerusalem, the policeman outside the church had set us up to get a guide (presumably for a share of the 100 shekels). Clearly set on getting us in and out of the church as fast as he could so he could get on to his next customers, the guide ushered us through to the site of the nativity via a back door. One of the pilgrims who had queued properly made a rude remark about queue-bargers, and I can't say I blame him. We were being swept along by a process we had failed to understand. I hadn't had an opportunity to get into the right frame of thinking about the site that I was about to see, and just felt uncomfortable at being there.

To be honest, Bethlehem for me had not been a spiritual experience, which was partly my own fault. We had packed so much in to our short trip without allowing for any compromises but in Bethlehem we got sucked into bribery, partly by being marked out because we were not part of an organised tour and partly because we were in a hurry. If I hadn't parted with some money we would not have seen anything so I rapidly changed from pilgrim to tourist which meant I was probably in the wrong frame of mind when we arrived at the manger. I will need to return at some point and queue to exorcise this mistake.

The Journey

When we returned to Manger Square our guide told us that he had already told our taxi driver that he could go and get his car and retrieve us. The four of us and the driver obviously stuck out like sore thumbs. The difficulties of this trip became more obvious as we then drove through Bethlehem. Moza had to push up my window (it had only been open by about three or four inches) when it became clear that some of the youth of Bethlehem were looking at our Israeli-plated Mercedes with not the friendliest of eyes.

We arrived at the Palestinian wall – and when I say 'wall' I mean a proper wall about twenty feet high and made of solid concrete, with barbed wire along the top and bullet proof towers – where Moza told us we should get out and cross by foot. He would meet us in the car on the other side. I asked him if he was joking. The only assurances we had were that we had got to know Moza a little bit and also that we had not yet paid our fare! But this was a rough place and we should not really have been there. Deborah and I had young children back in London and I am not sure we behaved particularly responsibly on this occasion. Once we had got out of the car we were pestered all along our route to the wall by two young teenage boys who were desperate for money, trying to sell us tin whistles and cards. They followed us the entire way until we left the Palestinian side. One of the boys then started to cry and so I went back and gave him a few shekels. We passed through the wall and into no-man's land between the Palestinian and Israeli sides. The two walls are approximately fifty yards apart but the entrances to each are not opposite each other so we had to find our way across to the Israeli wall with minimal sign posting. There, we were presented with heavy-duty security with soldiers behind bullet proof glass, but once through our driver quickly appeared around the corner to pick us up and whisk us back to Jerusalem.

It's difficult to describe the stark contrast between

the poverty of the Palestinian Territories and the lushness and wealth of Israel. Israel is like California. Britain is often described as the fifty-first state of the United States of America but if that is true then I think Israel is the fifty-second. The desert we drove through yesterday was arid in comparison to our journey back to the airport and the end of this third day: we passed through lush greenery, conifers, terraces, olives and vineyards on good roads travelled by big cars – I thought of it as a sort of 'California with history'. At one point we were overtaken by the Presidential cavalcade – a big Volvo with multiple security cars around it – and we wondered if the president would recognise our car from the previous day since he had also overtaken us as we had come in from Jericho. Even he was slowed down to a snail's pace at a roadblock, which to my mind suggested that his men hadn't got the security quite as they should have done. Kings, queens, presidents and prime ministers are not meant to get stuck in traffic jams!

Five miles away in Bethlehem or in the West Bank desert, people live in hovels with no water, subsisting on dry arid land with a few sheep. Rather than build the wall to keep everybody out perhaps the Israelis could have better spent their money on desalination plants to give the Palestinians water. The wall may work short term (and it does appear to have done – the number of suicide bombings has dropped markedly) but anybody who has read history knows that every wall built since Hadrian's Wall and the Great Wall of China has failed in its long-term purpose. The Jews need to cut their Arab neighbours into a slice of prosperity. Nothing could work better to isolate the lunatic Jihadists than to give the moderate majority a slice of the cake. I fully understand the fear and difficulties of the Israelis: suicide bombers and any other type of bomber are not welcome, of course, and I say this having been within four hundred yards of two

IRA bombs. I am also, if anything, pro-Israeli by political inclination but I am sure they are making a mistake here. This double wall with its pillboxes, no mans' land, barbed wire and soldiery behind bullet-proof and bomb-proof glass is a disaster in the making. This is how to make a nation feel like the oppressed, and the oppressed will always rise up at some point.

We finished our trip with a difficult passage through the multiple steps of security at Ben Gurion airport, where our bags were x-rayed, Gary's bags were searched, we were interviewed by security and, finally, faced a huge queue at passport control which almost made us miss our flight. We got on board with literally one minute to go. I was due back in the operating theatre in London the next morning.

Spirituality

As you know I am a gynaecological surgeon – to my mind this makes me a combination of surgeon, physician, and psychologist – and it is therefore with some trepidation that I write on themes of spirituality and religious belief. There are some, both within my profession and without, who hold that spirituality and religion should not be the domain of healthcare professionals at all, and I know that many of my colleagues shy away from the subjects in conversations with their patients, for fear of causing offence and losing their jobs. It's a tragically ironic situation when you consider that originally, in the Middle Ages, hospitals and healthcare were founded and run by religious organisations. Back then they were good at caring for the spirit and not particularly good at medicine, but now the situation is reversed: medicine delivers remarkable results but often without a sense of caring for the psychological and spiritual needs of the patient.

If you had asked me fifteen years ago to talk about my faith or any other faith I would have found that difficult. I would not have dared to say a word to anybody I worked with. But these days it's not that hard to discuss within the healthcare setting in which I work; I realise this may not be everybody's experience. However, many of the people with whom I work are quietly Christian or of other faiths.

Just the other day I had finished in theatre and had gone to the coffee room when one of the receovery team sat down next to me and pronounced 'Christ is risen, brother!'. It was orthodox Easter, and I have to say, I failed to make the correct orthodox response: 'He is risen indeed!', which I regret. And similarly with many of those I talk to – slowly I have realised that the majority are either church goers or actively pursuing other faiths. It is all quite rightly done very privately with no desire to cause offence to those of no faith. One of the nurses, Pat, a surgical assistant, recently left and I asked her what she was off to do. She said 'I'm going back to Scotland and I've only got two or three years before I retire. If you ever come to Stornaway look out for the Christian bookshop because I'm going to be running it!'

Before I write further about spirituality I should try to define what I mean by the term. For me, 'spirituality' means one's experience, or attempt to experience, a sense of the transcendental, either independent of religion or within the setting of a religious ceremony. The spiritual is as important a part of anybody's life as the religious and the psychological, and it is both independent of those two aspects and overlapping:

Despite this crossover between spirituality, religion and psychology, I'm surprised at how difficult it is to find teaching or writings that cross the boundaries between the three. There are plenty of psychologists who have written about psychology, and plenty of religious prelates and theologians have written on religion but few who will look beyond. One of the exceptions is the great Swiss psychologist, psychiatrist and mystic Carl Gustav Jung who in contrast made much study of this interaction of the three.

Jung coined the term individuation, by which he meant that a person had become psychoanalytically mature and psychologically separated from their parents. He perceived that this only happened when people reached their late thirties to early forties, and that until that point in our lives we are concerned with trying to get some sort of response (be it positive or negative) from our parents. This rings true for me – I know I individuated at around the age of thirty-eight, by which point in my life I had been a consultant for more than five years and had recently become Chief of Gynaecology at the Chelsea and Westminster Hospital. Whenever I went back to visit my parents at their house on the Isle of Bute, pre-dinner aperitifs would be served by my father. He would always ask me what I wanted and I would say, 'A sherry, please.' I didn't particularly like the drink – I would have preferred a beer – but I knew that wasn't the desired response so I asked for a sherry to please my father. At the age of thirty-eight I finally realized that while I cared very much for and about my parents and their welfare, this concern did not need to extend to my choice of aperitif! It was around this time that I finally became far less bothered about criticism of myself in my wider life. One is as one is! This was my point of individuation.

Jung also believed that at this point in one's life one starts to develop an interest in the question of why we are here on this planet. His book *Man in Search of a Soul* explores this – he was convinced that for the health of our psychological wellbeing it was essential that we all explore these issues. Where we get to with these questions is not the issue – what matters is that we have looked into it.

Jung also had some very interesting views on dreams ('The dream is the little hidden door in the innermost and most secret recesses of the psyche ... All consciousness separates; but in dreams we put on the likeness of that more universal, truer, more eternal man dwelling in the darkness of primordial night.') and believed in the collective subconscious – a place that can be entered by achieving a dream-like state or trance-like state. This is a state that can be achieved for some people through religious ceremonies, with a combination of ritual and chanting, and a mixture of sights, sounds and smells which have the capacity to induce a semi-hypnotic state. I will be writing more about this later in the book. Jung believed that the 'collective sub-conscious' was the explanation for 'synchronicity', the many coincidences in life that we all experience to a higher degree than chance would dictate. Life, according to Jung, was very much more than the series of random events that some rationalists would have us believe.

Clearly there are many paths through life, and different spiritual traditions seem to work for different people. We are all on the Journey and we will find and choose our own paths. My route over the last twenty years or so has been Christian, specifically the spirituality of Anglo-Catholicism, and so these are the experiences that I will be writing about in this book but I don't want to suggest that my path is in any way superior to anybody else's. It's just what works for me. I am well aware of the spirituality of Buddhism, having read much on this and also within Hinduism through various colleagues. I love the ceremony of Anglo-Catholicism and we certainly pray for the Pope, the ecumenical patriarch and the Archbishop of Canterbury. The High Mass to me is an amazing thing. I love the big processions, the festivals, the swinging of incense, the sense of mystery in the service, the liturgy ... Wow! It's difficult not to be moved by that sort of thing.

Spirituality

The Bible talks in various places about 'seeing the light': 'Your word is a lamp to my feet, and a light to my path,' says King David in the Psalms (Psalm 119:105), and in the Gospel of John, Jesus describes himself as 'the light of the world' (John 8:12). This can mean the light of understanding, of illuminating our path through life, but for me it also has a more literal interpretation: the seeing of the light of heaven has been central to some of the most formative moments of my own spiritual experience. I am well aware that many people I have spoken to have shared in similar experiences but are naturally reluctant to talk about them for fear of ridicule or worse. I have felt similarly until now, but have felt it important to share my experience in order to contextualise this book. For this I hope you will forgive me.

The first occasion – perhaps my first genuine 'spiritual' experience – came at the Kathara Monastery on the Greek island of Ithaca. I was going through my divorce at the time and felt at one of the lowest points in my life. I'd just fallen in with Gary and had become a regular churchgoer, and while on Ithaca I decided to climb up to see this monastery which sat on the saddle on a hill. I entered the monastery, alone, and all I recall was seeing as I just stood there was an incredible light – a heavenly light. It was a completely different experience to anything I'd felt before. A year later, I went back to Ithaca and visited the monastery again, but the experience was just not the same. I've been back many times since – we now go to Ithaca every year in the summer holidays – and I've sat and knelt in that church many times, but while it always feels really special I have never seen that amazing light there again.

Something similar happened to me a few years later in the former East German city of Leipzig, home for many years of the great composer Johann Sebastian Bach. I was there with a few friends and colleagues; on one day we had retired to a bar after a day's observing the great Professor

Höckel operating and, on impulse, I stood up and told them that I was going for a short wander. I knew that St Thomas Church, where Bach had been head of music, was just around the corner and as I had an interest in the music of this great genius I decided to take a look. I found the church fairly easily and, although it appeared to be empty, the door was open so I stepped inside. The church was indeed in almost complete darkness, but for a small dim light by the organ – a special organ built to resemble that which Bach himself would have used – where there was one other person, an organist who began to play. Now I'm not a big one for organ music but there is no other way of describing what I felt happened next, other than to say that the heavens opened and an enormous light filled the church. It was unlike any physical form of light that I had felt before, other than my experience in the Kathara Monastery, and I fell down on my knees and just started to cry. I couldn't stop crying. It was quite unbelievable and difficult to explain – I hadn't been in a particularly emotional state when I had entered the church, but this was an uncontrollable response to what I saw and felt around me.

Having had that experience once, well, it was a bit like in C S Lewis' *The Lion, the Witch and the Wardrobe* – I wanted to go back and find that little door in the back of the wardrobe again. I contrived quite rapidly to find another excuse to go to Leipzig, this time for a conference. In fact, I got to go twice – once to set up the conference and then for the event itself. On both occasions I went back to the church, but everything was different. The church was not in darkness, the colours weren't as I remembered them … it just wasn't the same, and I felt nothing similar to what I had experienced that first time. It was still a beautiful special place but the heavens did not open.

As a scientist and rationalist I often find myself asking

what is it that generates the overwhelming sense of the sacred in such places. These particular stories are unique to me but I know that millions of spiritual people around the world, and throughout human history, have had their own such moments of feeling close to a world beyond our own – everyone's own story will have been unique to them, yet together the sheer weight of direct experience suggests that there is something very real and important behind it all. Jung might have suggested the collective sub-conscious as an explanation for the particular sense of the sacred one can sometimes feel in holy sites. Certainly it is very difficult not to feel the weight of history, and of the faith of millions of people who have visited Jerusalem and many of the other holy sites that I will go on to describe in this book.

Richard Dawkins would have us believe such spiritual experience is all a fantasy, some form of collective madness, although whenever I hear him criticising religious belief I am reminded of Puddleglum the marshwiggle in another of C S Lewis's Narnia tales, *The Silver Chair*, who, when the witch says that Narnia is a fantasy, replies: 'If it is a fantasy then it is much better than the witch's reality and I will stick with the fantasy anyway'.

I am sure that that is a sentiment shared by many of my patients, particularly those who live with a cancer or other life-changing diagnosis. I would never claim that those with a spiritual side to their lives live longer, but I would venture to say that they perhaps live better. Their cup seems to veer to half full rather than half empty. A young woman whose cancer I had removed comes to mind. When we met at her six-week post-operative consultation, I showed her the Venn diagram demonstrating the overlap of spirituality, religion and psychology and asked whether any of the three areas appealed to her. She replied: 'Oh doctor, I'm a very spiritual person. My brother is a priest and I'm well into religion. And for good measure I've signed up with a psychologist!' Here was a woman who had really grasped what it was all about. I think that both she and I knew that while she was having a very tough time she would get through. And she did.

Assisi

Lord make me an instrument of your peace.
Where there is hatred let me sow love.
Where there is injury, pardon;
Where there is doubt, faith;
Where there is despair, hope;
Where there is darkness, light;
And where there is sadness, joy.

St Francis of Assisi

Day 1

It was a long Friday. I got up this morning after a disturbed night's sleep, not helped by the scrabbling of the children's guinea pigs in their hutch outside. Following breakfast with the children I left for my clinic at Charing Cross Hospital, conducting a short interview with the Mail on Sunday from my car en route. The newspaper had decided to run this weekend – for the first time in two or three years – an article on uterine transplantation, and I had already given them a longer interview the day before. I don't know yet whether their story will have a favourable angle, but I guess we'll find out on Sunday. I phoned my son to see how he got on in his Higher History. This is the first time in his Highers that he has sounded disappointed. Unfortunately the second paper had not proved good for him; it's to be hoped that it did not prove good for everybody else as well and that he'll still get a good result. No sooner had I arrived at the hospital than I was paged to be told by the nurse on duty in another of the hospitals that I work in that a post-operative patient from three days ago was bleeding heavily. There are few things more scary for a surgeon than one of one's post-op patients bleeding heavily, and the advice must always be to go to the nearest accident and emergency department, where unfortunately one will not able to sort it out oneself. I phoned the patient and was pleased and relieved to discover that she was probably having an early heavy period, possibly coupled with a urinary tract infection. This was easily dealt with.

The Friday morning clinic was the usual intense business involving lots of young people coming through with nasty diseases. This is always fairly draining but much more hairy if one has a flight to catch at the end of it. However, I made it to Heathrow by a quarter to two and met my travelling companion Andrew Wakeham-Dawson on the top floor of Terminal 5. We suffered our way through the evermore scrutinous process of security and, once through, felt finally able to kick off our pilgrimage in a seafood bar with the wonderful delicacy that is the Tsarina, a happy combination of blinis, sour cream, smoked salmon and caviar. It's not wholly in the spirit of St Francis, I admit, but truly delicious, particularly when washed down with a Bloody Mary for me and beer for Andrew (who had once, along with his wife Susie, had a very bad experience following Bloody Marys and consequently can never face one again).

Our flight was delayed because of difficulties with an air ambulance at Heathrow followed by an aborted take-off by another aircraft, so we arrived late at Rome Fiumicino Airport and then had to face huge queues at passport control. We would have been further delayed by at least another hour at the busy car hire desk, but here I had the advantage of an Avis Preferred Card which allowed us to go straight to the car park, get in our car and drive off with no queuing. The card is a freebie which I picked up on one of my American trips. When I reached the head of the queue at Philadelphia airport's Avis car hire, the woman behind the counter discovered that I was a doctor and said I was far too important to have waited so long, so gave me the preference card there and then. I was shocked: the medical profession are not used to this sort of consideration within the UK.

Our destination was the ancient Umbrian city of Spoleto, where we had a restaurant table pre-booked for just an hour and a quarter after the time that we finally managed to clear the airport. We had refused to pay an addition 35 Euros for Andrew to be on the driver's card, so he was lumbered with me being on driving duties there and back. I fear I gave him rather a white-knuckle ride as we careered along the main route into Rome and on to the *peripherique*, heading north towards Florence. It was the scenic route, or rather it would have been if it hadn't been about ten o'clock at night. We came within ten feet of taking the wrong turning to Terni, and naughtily I had to reverse back about fifteen yards up the hard shoulder to be able to turn off at the right place, but still we managed to shave a good twenty-five minutes off the normal travel time and we arrived in Spoleto only twenty minutes late, still in time for dinner at the restaurant below the hotel in the historic centre of the city, only fifty yards from a Roman amphitheatre. We tucked into a delicious meal of local delicacies washed down by local beer and Umbrian wine. The restaurant was originally Spoleto's first Franciscan monastery, dating back to the twelfth and thirteenth centuries. Things were far more primitive in my native Scotland back then, Robert the Bruce only defeating Edward II in 1314. When I've travelled I've realised the relative poverty of the Scots compared to many places elsewhere in the world, at least until the Victorian era when we started to make plenty of money.

On the wall opposite where we sat was a magnificent mural of Franciscan monks overlooking the amphitheatre, and on the staircase were further murals of San Damiano, the church which Francis was called to repair in his foundational vision of Christ. Spoleto was the site of Francis' first vision and so we had considered it an appropriate place from which to start our walk.

Day 2

We ended this day, Saturday, in a small *auberge* somewhere between Bazzano Superiori and Spoleto. Where were we meant to be? I don't know! Andrew and I had not booked anything; this was a pilgrimage tour, on which we needed to go with the flow, so wherever we ended up had to be right – that's the theory at least, happily proved correct on this occasion.

We had started the day by visiting Spoleto's tourist information bureau, expecting to find some high-quality walking maps of the St Francis route. Apparently there are no such maps. There were plenty of great maps for all the walks south of Spoleto, but nothing north to Assisi, bar a bicycle route map. We had a map that showed half of Italy on two pages that would have to do us. We bought some water and sunblock and made a brief visit to the amphitheatre before setting off on the main northern route out of town.

The first place of interest that we passed was a splendid cathedral, equal in grandeur to London's Brompton Oratory. Few other churches in the length and breadth of the British Isles could match the splendour found here in this provincial Italian town. It included a chapel painted by Leonardo Da Vinci, some great paintings including Daniel in the den of lions and Jerome writing the Vulgate Bible with his lion in tow, and a splendid San Damiano cross, one of the crosses (with the Tau cross) associated with Francis. As I walked past the cross a group of tourists arrived and one of them put some money in a slot which caused the cross to become suddenly and startlingly illuminated. I returned to the cross when they had left, and knelt on the *prie dieu* (a prayer desk) for a couple of minutes.

As we left the cathedral we noticed a sign for the St Francis walk. So it did exist! I was relieved for as long as it took us to follow the direction of the sign and reach a dead end. We asked directions and were told to take a certain route which also turned out (after five miles) to be the wrong direction. At this point we realised that we had lost our only decent map so Andrew hurtled off back down the hill to try and find it, probably adding a good two miles to his day. While I waited for him I sat down by the side of the road with my book. Italians are caring people and many slowed down and made sure I wasn't in any trouble. Andrew eventuall reappeared, lathered in sweat and in need of huge quantities of water, but he did at least have the map. We realised that if we continued up the hill we were on, we would be able to then take a route down a dirt track to Poleto, which we anticipated we might reach by evening.

We had by now ascended about two thousand feet, and were blessed with splendid panoramic views down the Umbrian valley. We stopped and looked down on a disused railway track and a new motorway that ran underneath the mountain that we were walking over. Such is progress: the Victorians built railways, we build motorways. After some hesitation, we found the route down to Poleto as we thought, but at some point – in fact, probably more than once – we took the wrong turn and ended up on a very steep slope, utilising no path whatsoever. Our walk through the woods was much coloured by seeing various butterflies, and at one point I heard heavy movement in the undergrowth and thought I had seen a Muntjac deer but it turned out to be several wild boar. At this point I handed Andrew one of my walking sticks, which both have decent spikes on them, and retrieved my hunting knife from the rucksack. You are unlikely to be attacked by wild boar unless you have cornered one. However, some weaponry seemed to be a good idea at this juncture.

The Journey

Eventually we arrived at a small place called Bazzano Inferiori, which was not where we had expected to be. We thought we were far further across the mountains than we actually were. At this point we had walked fifteen miles and probably only covered about six or seven as the crow flies. We heard bells ringing above us and marched up the hill to Bazzano Superiori, with every expectation of finding there a beautiful piazza next to the church, full of Italian families eating and drinking. Unfortunately the place was deserted and it transpired there was no restaurant, no bar, nothing!

An elderly lady told us there was a place a few kilometres away and we vacillated over whether to take the pilgrim route or the road, ultimately deciding to take the road in case we found a restaurant along the way. In fact, the road turned out to be the pilgrim route, on which we met two more women, a mother and daughter. In my best, but highly limited, Italian, I asked '*Dove est ristorante?*' '*100 metri,*' replied the mother, gesticulating left, and then '*200 metri,*' gesticulating right. Our luck had come good at last.

Dinner was our first meal since breakfast, having snacked on just nuts and some oat bars high up in the hills. The food was good and we drank hefty quantities of beer. When we had arrived at the hotel there were no other guests but by half-way through our meal the restaurant was packed with Italian farmers and their families enjoying their Saturday night out, and a great evening was had by all. We were the only diners who did not have to find their way home. Our pleasantly decorated rooms had lovely views down the valley. It had been a cloudy day with a little light rain on occasions, and I had found it similar to walking in the West of Scotland with a fine sunset to match. Umbria has a much softer landscape, however. This is where the Etruscans lived, and where the Romans had followed them. This is also where Francis travelled after his conversion experience, nine hundred years before us.

Day 3

This morning we were back on the pilgrimage path by a quarter past nine, and we managed a whole half mile before our first wrong turn of the day – a three-way split in the road with no signposts – not rediscovering the pilgrimage route for a further seventeen miles. We had seen the day as a practical exercise in getting ourselves down the valley near to Monte Subasio, a four thousand foot climb and a three and a half thousand foot drop which we would climb the following day, and as it happened we accidentally skirted Poreta, passed below the hilltop town of Trevi and eventually found a rest opposite the *duomo* cathedral in Foligno. We would sleep that night in the ancient town of Spello, just a few miles further north up the road. The day had felt less pilgrimage and more of a route march – we were on asphalt the whole way and had sore feet by the time we reached our destination.

We checked into a 2-star *auberge* in the mountain town of Spello, a medieval town nestled on the flank of Monte Subasio which we intended to climb the following day. There was a wedding party below the rooms where we were staying and a light aircraft went by, performing a barrel roll just above the hotel for the benefit of the bride and groom. Andrew had told me earlier on that the day was the feast of Pentecost, marking the transformation of Jesus' disciples from a timorous group of men and women into highly motivated preachers. During the afternoon I had been able to look at one of my favourite books which I regularly carry with me on my travels, *The Subjects of Early Russian Icons*, and cross-reference it with the relevant Bible passages in the copy of the New Testament that I also keep with me. If you are into icons, *The Subjects of Early Russian Icons* is a fantastic book and conveniently portable, measuring just three by two inches, with a picture of an icon plus explanation on each double page. I had by now collected most of the icons illustrated but one that I didn't have was the icon of the Pentecost, illustrating the Holy Spirit as described in the Book of Acts, coming down upon the disciples after Jesus had ascended and enabling them to understand and speak all languages. St Peter commented that the disciples were 'speaking in tongues' rather than just drunk (which wasn't true of Andrew and me at the end of this day – at least, that's what Deborah told me when I phoned her just before going off to sleep).

On a more serious note however, it transpires that this speaking in tongues was designed to satisfy a prophecy from the Book of Joel:

> *'And it shall come to pass in the last days saith god, I will pour out of my spirit upon all flesh; And your sons and your daughters shall prophesise, and your young men shall see visions, and your old men shall dream dreams.'*
> Acts 2:17

The last few words of this passage is a significant quote for me personally. My father was a professional after-dinner speaker who toured the globe, at his peak delivering fifty speeches a year (plus around ten Burns' Supper events). Shortly before my fortieth birthday the gauntlet had been thrown down to me to follow in his footsteps. Father was president of a group in Glasgow called the Nomads – a highly prestigious group of professional and business people from the West of Scotland. He had been preceded in this role many years earlier by such luminaries as Sir Compton Mackenzie, of

Whisky Galore fame, and others. The tradition at their events was for the president to speak, followed by a nominated guest, for between fifteen and thirty minutes, to present the audience with a serious message and amuse them without being vulgar. I was nominated to second my father, on the theme of 'Your young men shall see visions, and your old men shall dream dreams'. I prepared my speech at a speed of about two hours per spoken minute, using for inspiration the work of Carl Gustav Jung, his belief that dreams are the 'hidden door' to the recesses of one's subconscious, and the requirement to integrate religion and spirituality back into medicine. It seemed to go down well with my audience, and is a theme that deeply underlies my reasons for wanting to write this book you are reading today.

Day 4

This was some day, as we walked from Spello to Assisi, via the daunting climb of Mount Subasio. We had a later than normal start to the day, due to the effects of the night before, stepping outside to a cool, cloudy morning – it had been a clear night on which one could see the hills behind Spolleto away on the horizon, but now in daylight, visibility was about half that distance although some gentle sunlight played over green fields dotted with oak trees. Our hotel overlooked an ancient medieval church with a rectangular courtyard bordered on three sides by huge Cypress trees. An elderly Italian couple tended their garden on the terrace above, but this was a quiet town which didn't seem used to having walking tour visitors. The manager of our hotel lived and worked in Spello, and was based at the top of the town and therefore closest to the start of the route to Monte Subasio, yet even he had no idea where that was.

We found our bearings though and duly started our slow but steady assent, accompanied by a cat for the first five hundred yards until we reached a Roman aqueduct. I had always thought of aqueducts as large structures like viaducts, this was a much smaller stone structure with the run off for the water approximately six inches across in a rectangular shape, not dissimilar to the bore of the pipes that the London Water Board (inconveniently) appear to be installing around our streets at the moment.

Our climb took us initially through olive groves then through heath land and into pine forests. Andrew is something of a polymath – knowledgeable not only about religion, agriculture and military history, but also possessing the ability to name virtually every flower that I pointed at, not to mention every tree, every insect and every bird, which he could also identify just from their song. I remember hearing a fascinating piece on BBC Radio 4 about how birds learn their songs from their parents, and that as subsequent generations rarely move geographically the bird song you might hear standing, say, on a specific farm on the North Yorkshire moors, would be the same song that your grandparents would have heard if they stood in the same place eighty years earlier. This, as Andrew pointed out, is the equivalent of how geographical human dialect works. Of course humans move a lot more these days, but many of us keep our dialects even when we do move; as the saying goes, 'You can take the man out of Glasgow, but you cannot take Glasgow out of the man,' although this probably refers to more than just dialect and accent!

The pine forest gradually became oak forest and ash forest with a very similar topography and botany to what one might find back in the UK, until we eventually broke out above the tree line to an open area with a fresh water spring and a small bothy. We sat down for an impromptu picnic of Andrew's biscuits and spreads, all a minimum of four years out of date. I feel certain health and safetypeople would have forbidden us to eat it, notwithstanding the fact that there was absolutely nothing wrong with any of it – followed by Mini Crunchies, Flakes and Chocolate Caramels. We looked like an advert for Cadbury! My children will probably be quite angry with me if they ever read this as I pinched the chocolates from their cupboard before I left. If you've ever wondered which chocolate is most suitable for pilgrimage walking then forget about Flakes as what comes out is a chocolate powder that gets everywhere, and Chocolate Caramels are also very messy. Make sure that you have a fresh water spring nearby to wash your hands.

Duly satisfied, we headed off again up the mountain and soon encountered a quite remarkable transformation in the general topography. Monte Subasio from a distance appears to be a great big grass-covered mound somewhat like the South Downs but once we were actually on it we discovered it covered in wild flowers, juniper bushes and high alpine pasture. There were many horses and mules grazing up there, most likely used for work with lumber in the correct season, and lots of people too, with baskets and umbrellas, shuttling around across the green grass looking for something (which we later discovered, through a conversation in broken Italian with three women, to be wild mushrooms).

New vistas, with more high mountains in the distance, opened up for us to the north and west as we crossed further pastures below some radio masts and discovered two craters which we thought at first must be volcanic in origin. We later discovered that the top of the mountain is actually quite porous, and with water ingress these two pits – approximately two hundred feet wide by sixty to one hundred feet deep – have developed over the years and then grassed over. They would certainly be something to avoid in winter when the snow would be knee deep; with a pack on I think one would struggle to ever get out – a bad way to go!

We reached the summit, enjoyed spectacular views, and then, shortly after starting our descent, came across a solitary wooden cross which was sitting on a shoulder of rock, from which we got our first sight of Assisi: a truly splendid and stirring picture of sandstone buildings spilling down a hillside punctuated by multiple churches, battlements and towers.

Our route took us next down a valley populated by cows with calves, which made me wary as cows with young to protect have a tendency to charge. A few weeks ago in Bute a cow with calves came charging at me across a field at such speed that I thought she was going to jump the fence and try to gore my father's old dog, Tamino, who I regularly walked with. This would have created much difficulty since I would have felt duty bound to try and protect Tamino, but fortunately it screeched to a halt at the last second. In the high pastures of Montesubasio neither the cows with calves nor the bull that was also in the herd, showed any such interest in us, and after stopping for water we were able to continue our descent through very steep, canopied woodland (in the winter I am sure there would have been a big stream running to our right) until we reached the Hermitage of St Francis.

This was a splendid monastery with two Franciscans in charge. '*Silenzio*' was requested on multiple signs as we approached on a track of fine stones and entered a beautiful courtyard with English-scented roses, geraniums and other potted plants sitting on top of walls. A little shop run by a monk sold candles, and on the other side of the tiny courtyard there was a small refectory through which one could see a chapel, where Francis and the other brothers used to eat. A sign took us to two further chapels and then down an increasingly narrow staircase into a small cave, with a claustrophobic yet very holy atmosphere, where Francis used to live alone and pray. Beyond this were various statues of Francis and other brothers in positions of prayer and a large wooden cross with an altar around which sat a few Italian people, but we decided not to walk further, as I was slightly nervous about having left my rucksack with the entirety of my belongings back up in the courtyard. Back at the hermitage we had a coffee and decided not to wait the half hour until the next chapel service as we still had another hour and a half's steep downhill walking to Assisi ahead of us.

We finally entered Assisi through the city's north gate. 'Good Camino!' (a reference to the Santiago de Compostelo pilgrimage), shouted a beer-drinking man as we strode into one of the main squares high up in the town. Our rucksacks were dangling with compasses, water bottles, binoculars, sunglasses and various other accoutrements that clearly – and gratifyingly – marked us out as serious walkers to this man, who turned out to be the only other walker we encountered in our entire fifty plus miles of pilgrimage.

I had thought that I'd arranged us a hotel in the heart of the city but the topography is confusing as Assisi cascades down perhaps seven to eight hundred feet of hillside, and the main cathedral near which I had booked our stay is at the bottom not, as I had in my mind, at the top. So it was a bit of a walk to get there but it proved to be a comfortable venue and we had a drink on its balcony before heading out for a pizza. We had been enjoying a fairly carnivorous diet but decided to go for something a little lighter after the day we had just had: according to the pedometer we had only clocked up fifteen miles but expended a huge quantity of energy climbing and ascending, probably more than the previous day after which our feet had been much sorer.

Day 5

The day began with a quick return to Spolleto to pick up the hire car, then back to Assisi. We struck lucky as the hotel's Albanian porter offered to drive us there, saving the need for a taxi or a train ride followed by another big walk. I reckoned he had a minor case of *delirium tremens* as he kept twitching and looking as though he was trying to rub insects off himself as he drove along. The sisters (blood, not religious) who ran our Spolleto hotel had kept our bags, and my filofax in their safe, so we picked up those before collecting the car, noticing as we did so that Italian car parks are far more agreeable than British ones: there is no smell of urine, and the lifts work! The more trips abroad one takes, the more one has to wonder the arrogant British assumption that we do things far better than anyone else. Our drive back to Assisi took just three-quarters of an hour along a fast dual carriageway, and it was satisfying to know that we'd already covered the entirety of this ground by a much more circuitous route.

Before parking up in Assisi we visited two of the shrines for Francis. One, at Sancturia Rivotorto, was the place where he and the original brothers had lived in a pig sty, and the other, was at the San Damiano church, the site of the original church where a vision of Christ had clearly and resonantly pierced Francis' soul: 'Francis, go now and repair my church which as you see is falling down.' The command applied both physically to the crumbling church of San Damiano and metaphorically to the wider Church of Francis' time. Francis' original conversion experience had occurred in Spolleto when he was on his way to join the Crusades and God spoke to him in a dream, asking him whom he was really serving. To great opprobrium from his fellow townsmen he turned back to Assisi, city of his birth, gave away his fine clothes, rejected his father and started living with the poor and sick. Francis practised an almost Buddhist type of Christianity – the statue of him on the approach to San Damiano looks just like the Buddha, deliberately styled so I am sure – and his love of all things and all people shines through. There many moving stories of his life and work, his compassion to the sick and contagious and to wild and dangerous animals.

Back in Assisi, we spent the final afternoon of our trip wandering through the streets and visiting the various shrines. I chose to go down all the side chapels in the upper basilica of the cathedral before dipping down into Francis's tomb, a very moving place which was hidden until relatively recently, and full of praying pilgrims. Upstairs I went to the main altar of the cathedral and then came out through a back staircase onto a courtyard and roof area where I discovered a fantastic museum of medieval and renaissance ecclesiastical art.

From there we returned to the top of the city, to another cathedral, not the main basilica but one built on old Roman remains, that we had seen when we first came into town on foot. There, in a side chapel, we partook of Vespers with some nuns and then stayed for Mass, although I think the priest was somewhat dubious about both Andrew's and my qualifications to be at his service: we were not covered to the wrist, merely to above the elbow – clearly influenced by NHS infection control policies!

Our final stop of the day was at a little chapel whose rotunda roof I had spied with my binoculars from the saddle of the hill by the wooden cross, two thousand feet higher up the previous day. It turned out to be the cell into which Francis's father, Pietro Bernadone, put him in and chained him up after beating him as a little boy. The father's own chambers above on the other side of the church were locked. This gave me my first proper insight into why and how Francis so thoroughly rejected his father and followed a path into rags and hair shirt. Bernadone has certainly had bad press over the years (less so Francis' mother, the Lady Pica, to whom there was a monument outside the chapel), and quite deservedly. I find it quite inconceivable why anyone would want to beat their children. Contrary to current politically correct thinking, I do think the odd smack does no harm depending on the type of child one has. I have four children myself, two of whom have only ever been smacked perhaps twice each, while the other two have failed to respond to any form of logical argument or, as I would describe it, normal punishment such as being sent to sit on the naughty step. Aged just three, one of my children absolutely refused to do this in very rude terms – at this sort of point one realises that one is running out of options and a sharp tap on the hand may do no harm. However, being beaten and placed in chains as Francis was would quite rightly get the social workers round, followed by a swift appearance in court and transfer to jail, so some aspects of society at least have got better with time.

We meandered back down through the shops, of which there were many (Assisi is a sort of 'Jerusalem lite' when it comes to shopping), to our hotel, where we finished our trip with a decent meal looking down the valley to the church commemorating where Francis died.

As I look back on this trip the part which really sticks out is the visit to the hermitage high on the hill, above all the grandeur that is Assisi. That for me represented the heart of the St Francis story. When we had emerged from the hermitage and retrieved our backpacks we met a group of nuns, and were addressed in Italian by their Mother Superior (a superior woman in many ways). I said that we didn't speak Italian, that we were Scottish and English. She asked me from where I came from in Scotland; I usually just say Glasgow for simplicity's sake but on this occasion I told the exact truth – Falkirk, which for the record is half way between Glasgow and Edinburgh. The Mother Superior said one of the sisters in her nunnery came from Falkirk and she then gave us a Blessing. This was very special and alone would have been worth all the walking on our trip.

Jerusalem

The author and his wife Deborah, with the Dome of the Rock behind us.

Inside the Church of the Holy Sepulchre.

Jerusalem

Robert Chandler is the mote in the Eye of the Needle!

The author enjoying shopping on the streets of Jerusalem.

Assisi

The author at the start of the path over Monte Subassio.

A statue of St Francis, sitting in a position we more commonly associate with Buddha.

Andrew Wakeham-Dawson on the upper slopes of Monte Subassio.

Athos

St Paul's Monastery at the foot of Athos.

Iona

Holy Isle and Arran, as seen from Garroch Head, Bute.

Iona

Arran as seen from Bute.

A view of Iona.

Patmos

The Monastery of St John the Divine.

A private chapel on Patmos.

Patmos

The beach of Psili Ammos.

The author on the roof of the Monastery of St John. The chapel of the Prophet Elias can be seen on the horizon.

Pilgrimage

U ntil I discovered pilgrimage I had no idea of the great variety of ways of being a pilgrim, nor that there can be many different motivations for being so. Some people choose to go to places of healing such as Lourdes, some to places of significance from the Bible and some to the sites associated with the saints. Some go in search of those Celtic 'thin places' – a place on earth at which one feels tangibly closer to God – that I described earlier in the book. Some people go on pilgrimage in large groups, some in small groups, some with just one companion and others alone. Pilgrimage can be done by car or by bus or by any mode of transport, although what I write about in this book is primarily pilgrimage by walking, allowing for the practice of a combination of exercise, chant and trance.

My first pilgrimage, although I didn't realise it as such at the time, was to Rome with Deborah and Gary, where we had a splendid weekend seeing many of the sites under Gary's wonderful guidance. The first trip that I planned *as* a pilgrimage was to Mount Athos, a destination hankered for by the pilgrim in *The Way of a Pilgrim* as his spiritual advisor had instructed him to follow the teachings of an Athonite book, the *Philokalia*.

My two visits to Athos with Andrew Wakeham-Dawson have incorporated some of the most personally significant days of my life, for in that ancient repository of the spirit of Byzantium *The Way of the Pilgrim* truly came to life for me. We have walked for many miles on that Holy Mountain and I for one felt that I had been transported into a world from the writings C S Lewis, or J R R Tolkein.

Mount Athos is a forty-mile long peninsula of northern Greece, cut off from the outside world by a high barbed-wire fence and only accessible by boat. Legally it is a separate republic within the state of Greece so one needs to present oneself at the offices of the Holy Executive in Thessalonica to obtain one's travel permit. Then, following a two-hour drive across to Ouronopolis, which loosely translates as 'the gate of heaven', one gets one's permit stamped at the passport office, allowing the purchase of a boat ticket to Mount Athos. This might not be a pilgrimage on which many of my readers will be able to follow in my footsteps because among the rules for visiting the monastic republic are that it is male only, and within that restriction are allowed no unbearded youth, no swimming and no wearing of shorts!

The first visit was pre-planned, with bookings made to stay at various monasteries on the mountain, then for the second visit we left our sleeping arrangements completely to chance fully aware that we might end up in a ditch for the night, if circumstances didn't go our way. As well as the Greeks, the Russians, Serbs, Bulgarians and Romanian Orthodox orders all have monasteries on the island – all huge medieval fortresses whose gates shut at sun down – so there were numerous places for us to find to stay as long we got our timings right. The monasteries themselves are variable in their levels of luxury as the monks all live very frugally. We stayed in places with no mirrors, no electricity and no cold water but always received a very warm welcome from the monks. To be fair, we also stayed in one or two places which could easily have been four star hotels, some with a warm welcome and one with no welcome at all!

We were a little skeptical of the place on our first visit, but returned convinced of the great holiness of Athos. The monks make thousands of pilgrims welcome every year, and are usually very generous in allowing us into the main parts of most of their religious services. Their longer religious services are conducted in Byzantine chant and, while rather disgracefully I speak virtually no Greek, I find it relatively easy to get into the groove. There is one service in particular, in an Iviron monastery, that sticks in my memory. It started badly for me as I had entered the church at four o'clock in the morning when it was pitch dark and mistakenly headed for a seat (the seats being in the style of booths) but mistakenly sat down on an elderly monk! Having made my apologies I found an empty seat and began to get into the repetitive chant of the service. Suddenly, at about five o'clock, the whole church was lit up by the first rays of sun striking down through the dome in the roof, illuminating the monastery's huge fresco of Christ Pantocrator. Wow, do these monks know a thing or two! It was an incredible sight.

We discovered another very generous group of monks at St Paul's Monastery, a vast medieval structure. Andrew and I had set off early from the monastery of Stavronikita, hoping to walk, hitch a lift to the southern end of the peninsula and then climb up into the area known as the desert where hermits live. As luck would have it, two young monks stopped their four-wheel drive vehicle and asked us if we wanted a lift. We asked where they were going, to which they replied to St Paul's. This was the other side of the peninsula from where we had planned to go that day, but in the spirit of going with the flow we took them up on their offer, leading to the most spectacular journey up over the peninsula below Mount Athos. The vehicle slithered about in the snow, with vertiginous drops to one side.

When we got to St Paul's, the monks ran into a *skete* (a small monastic community, in which they lived), and brought us back a cake that they had baked. We thanked them profusely and then started our walk to approach the desert from the west side rather than the east. We walked for eight hours round the side of the mountain, reaching a height of about three thousand feet, before rounding a corner to realise with some horror that we were still about a mile away from where we wanted to be, but to get there would have involved going back down to sea level and up again. This was beyond us for the day, so we turned tail and headed back down the hill all the way to St Paul's, where we literally staggered through the gates just before they closed. The guest master took one look at us and sent us into the refectory where we were fed and watered and then joined by some monks who wanted to chat to us about football (about which they knew more than Andrew and me put together). Eventually we were given a room in which we slept for hours. Here was true hospitality. You are not able to pay for your hospitality in monasteries; it is freely given, and in that particular monastery with genuine love for the pilgrim.

I know that at least half of my readers are likely to be women, and are therefore not able to visit Mount Athos, although there is an area nearby which has nunneries operating to a similar regimen. Much closer to home, however, is the Athonite monastery of Tolleshunt Knight, in the wilds of Essex, which was founded in the 1950s. There is a monastery with three churches on one side of a country road, and on the other side a nunnery with two more churches. About fifty monks and nuns live there, separately but sharing some meals and their resources. The issue of men and women in holy orders and how to mix them, if at all, is vexed one, but I think the Tolleshunt Knight set-up seems to work well. On Mount Athos itself, I do believe that the all-male nature of the place, while I know it upsets some, is essential to its current working, and I'm sure the same applies to the nearby nunneries.

I have not yet undertaken two of the best-known Christian pilgrimage walks – the *Camino* to Santiago de Compostello and the *Via Francigena* from Canterbury to Rome by way of Reims, Lausanne and the St Bernard's Pass (although the St

Pilgrimage

Francis route that I sought in Assisi makes up a small part of this). Ironically the *Camino* has been a favourite pilgrimage for many of my patients, but one of the difficulties – for me at least – with these longer walks is finding the time to do them. The *Camino* is variable in length depending where you start and which route you take and I know many who have split it up and done sections over a week at a time, but to do the walk in one go all the way from Paris to Santiago is a two- to three-month undertaking – one of my patients did complete this, post-surgery and chemotherapy. Some people may be able to manage twenty to twenty-five miles per day over a period of three or four days, but for any longer period the expert advice is to aim for a maximum of fifteen miles per day, six days a week, with one day of rest. Failure to follow this sort of regimen generally leaves people unable to walk at all because of blisters, joint pain and torn muscles.

For long distance walking it is more likely that one will be able to get in the spiritual groove if travelling alone or with just one companion. In especially remote places having a companion makes good common sense for safety reasons alone. Just the other day I was out walking alone in the Scottish mountains and there was a point at which I wondered what the hell I was doing there because I was stuck in a gulley when a howling blizzard hit. I could hardly walk forwards, had no radio contact and was completely alone – if I'd twisted my leg up there I'd have been in a lot of trouble. Fortunately I managed to climb out but it was a risk I shouldn't have taken. At the very least, if you are going to walk alone make sure somebody else knows exactly where you are going so that they'll know where to look for you if you don't come back!

If you are to do it as a two, then it's important to give careful consideration to choosing the right companion – make sure that it's somebody you will be happy to spend a number of days with, and that you're compatible not only in terms of what you can accomplish physically but also at a personal and spiritual level.

If there is anything that this pilgrimage has taught me over and above all the others, is it the value of silence. Andrew and I are good at moving in and out of each other's company and giving each other space, sometimes walking long distances a few hundred yards apart. I have spent an awful lot of my life surrounded by noise, talking and music. I love music: I have a CD player with headphones, and speakers that I can use in hotel rooms. It is only relatively recently come to see the value of having no noise at all. Silence really can be golden.

Interestingly, my sister Alison and my nineteen-year-old daughter Victoria vehemently disagree with my assertion of the value of silence during walking. Having read the first draft of the manuscript for this book Alison wrote the following comments which I want to include to provide a different perspective: 'Richard believes in chanting at times and quiet contemplation; my pals and I chant all the time but to each other. We know each other's lives in depth having walked and talked together for the last six years on a regular basis. We sort each other out but it is not the same as sitting round a table. Maybe it's the fact that you have little eye contact with each other as you struggle up a Munro (any Scottish mountain over 3000 feet high) in a gale, but you share far more than usual. Exercise and chat do it for me, they have given me my best experiences, although endorphins and fighting the elements do help also. I am not keen on Munros but the exhilaration at the top, with a view, is the very best feeling – that is when I feel near to God even though I am not religious.'

In my experience a pilgrimage taken as part of a larger group usually turns out to be a very different experience from one taken as just a one or two. For my fiftieth birthday I aimed to replicate part of Chaucer's Canterbury Tales with a group of family and friends (to Canterbury from Rochester rather than all the way from London but it was still forty miles over two days, staying in an old coaching inn overnight) and we soon fell into much partying. It was great fun but there was little chant and trance! My son was introduced to 'beer bonding' perhaps a little too young! The spirit of Chaucer was firmly around :

> *When Spring is in the air*
> *People long to go on*
> *Pilgrimages ...*

Or to quote the original:

> *When that April with his shoures soote,*
> *The droughte of March hath pierced to the roote,*
> *Thanne longen folk to go on pilgrimages ...*

Three years later Alison did the St Cuthbert's walk from Melrose to Lindisfarne for her own fiftieth birthday – a 'girls only' walk with the husbands and children joining in for the last day, on which we all covered about twenty miles to reach the Holy Isle. Lindisfarne definitely qualifies as one of those Celtic thin places and it haunts my memories still now.

Each separate pilgrimage that one takes is its own journey but many taken over the course of years will be joined together within you to form a wider single journey. In this book I have tried to demonstrate a personal journey – a development of ideas and some spiritual formation – that occurred in me over the course of four pilgrimages: to Jerusalem, Assisi, Iona and Patmos.

These trips – indeed all I have undertaken – have made deep impressions on me. For the first few days after my return from each I could think of little else when not at work. You will be pleased to know that the nature of my work precludes thinking about much other than work when I'm there! Monday, Thursday, Friday and alternate Wednesdays are taken up with clinics. I usually start at eight o'clock and work, without a break except for maybe fifteen minutes at lunch, through to seven in the evening. People have waited many weeks for their appointments and it does not matter where in the day they are, they need my full attention. My formula is to take the patient's history, summarise the issues, examine the patient, order the investigations and formulate the management plan. With twelve to sixteen patients every day this is intensive and can be pretty draining. Poor Deborah often gets no conversation out of me when I get home. Tuesdays and the alternate Wednesdays are my operating days, which are different. They start with the day's smallest cases (allowing those patients to get home earlier) and build upwards in intensity. Perhaps surprisingly I quite often find my mind on other things, especially during the big cases. Apparently the occupational psychologists say this is a sign of high competence – I hope so! Often during theatre in my head I find myself walking the hills of Bute, wandering round Iona or Mount Athos, or climbing the hills on Patmos.

Iona

Deep peace of the running wave to you
Deep peace of the flowing air to you
Deep peace of the quiet earth to you
Deep peace of the shining stars to you
Deep peace of the Son of Peace to you

Celtic prayer

δay 1

This was my third trip to Iona in two years. The first time I came with my two older children. We had stood in my parents' house, where there is a large painting of Iona, and promised ourselves that we would swim in the bay. In fact, we swam in the wrong bay, but it was still very beautiful. What draws one back to Iona? Partly, this time round, a desire to please Deborah; partly to please myself; and partly a desire to let Gary and Robert see this place, which must be Scotland's holiest.

The second runner for that title has to be St Andrews, the next pilgrimage walk that we have planned. But St Andrews is the Scottish equivalent of Canterbury before the Reformation. Iona is where it – that is, Christianity – all started in Scotland.

We had collected Gary and Robert early that morning from Gary's vicarage in Little Venice, and enjoyed a first-class British breakfast of bacon, eggs, mushrooms and all sorts of goodies at Gordon Ramsay's Plane Food at Heathrow's Terminal 5. From there we had an uneventful flight to Glasgow, picked up our car hire and drove onwards to Loch Lomond, one of the great jewels in the environs of Glasgow – a majestic stretch of water with the mountains beyond. We progressed from there to Inveraray, clan seat of the Campbells. I had been there a few months ago with my parents, and lunched at the George Hotel – a fine hostelry and a favourite stopping-off point years ago when I used to go to Tarbert, Loch Fyne for Hogmanay. Many a pint of ale has been consumed at the George Hotel, and many a man and woman fallen ill on the remainder of the drive to Tarbert. The receptionist, an ex-

The Journey

Glasgow police woman, had recognised Dad, who had been Senior Sheriff of Glasgow for many years, with a ferocious reputation for dispensing hard but fair justice.

The night before our departure on this current trip to Iona I had had a conversation with my father which, as I put the phone down, made me realise how blind one can sometimes be to that which is obvious. It's almost as if the closer something is, the harder it is to see. In our conversation he said he was feeling tense. I think a lot of elderly people whose world has shrunk to a degree feel this way. That evening I suddenly realised that old age is like the cancer conundrum: it is a feeling of impending mortality and the challenge of how to live in the present while not becoming dysfunctional worrying about a future of uncertain duration. The solution for the elderly has to be the same as it is for cancer patients: they need to develop strategies to see the world more positively – to live in the here and now.

An old man with a newspaper
Sits huddled at a table there.

Alone with all the noise around.
He thinks abject in age's fears
How little he enjoyed the years

When he was strong and sane and sound.
He understands he's old; he knows
And yet the time of youth still glows –
How short the road! – like yesterday.
He trusted Prudence – how absurd! –
She tricked him with a lying word:
'Plenty of time. Another day.'
Ardour restrained, the sacrifice
Of joy – to have been vainly wise

Is mocked by every chance that's gone …
But with his thoughts and memories deep
Presently dazed he falls asleep

Over the table all alone.

This slightly uncomfortable poem by C P Cavafy is, I believe, apposite for us all. *Carpe diem* is the way forward. Seize the day! I have reproduced it here less in relation to my father than to myself and my own fears. Over the years, my father has seriously stepped up to the plate. In his eighties, to great acclaim, he published his autobiography which ran to two editions. He and my mother have continued to extend a warm welcome to an ever-burgeoning extended family, which visits on rotation throughout the year, keeping us all close. My children all love going to Grandma and Grandpa's!

On this occasion we chose not to stop in Inveraray but took the right turn for Loch Awe. Gary drew an appreciative gasp as we came over the hill to be faced with a dramatic juxtaposition of water, sky and mountains – the horizon dominated by Ben Cruachan. Circling around the eastern end of the loch, we drove up to St Conan's church. This is a remarkable, not-so-little church that had been built in the 1930s and, although Presbyterian, fashioned in the French style with a large nave, altar and choir stalls, and cloisters off to the side. There are three reliquary chapels, one of which displays a bone of King Robert the Bruce. The overall effect is Catholic to say the least. The West Highland train line runs just below the gardens of the church, and below this lies the loch. We soaked up the atmosphere, I climbed to the war memorial higher in the grounds and we bought some postcards.

We arrived in Oban on a stunning summer's day that had drawn out large crowds of tourists – a happy contrast from the last time I'd been through, when Oban was looking somewhat down-at-heel compared to my memories of childhood and teenage years. One of my memories involved coming here with my grandparents and travelling to the islands on the King George V steamer – a redoubtable boat that ended up as a bar on the Thames. My Grandfather Richards was an enthusiastic photographer and used to show my sister Alison and I bedtime slide shows of his and Grandma's extensive travels. In 1964 they had travelled around the world for a whole year, sending back cards twice a week and returning with literally thousands of photos. We plotted their course on a world map on the bedroom wall at home. I was sent the front page of an American newspaper reporting that Grandpa Richards had gone over the Niagara Falls in a barrel. Alison and I believed it, and I only realised it had been a joke later in life!

We parked near the ferry terminal and walked through the town in the direction of the Oban Episcopalian Cathedral of St John the Divine, a typical red sandstone structure which sadly looked as though it had been experiencing some structural problems. A serious amount of iron work was holding it up from the inside out. Gary recalled that Oban Cathedral had always been Anglo-Catholic. For the uninitiated, this means that it looks, feels and smells 'High Church'. Now it still had a splendid altar but appeared to have gone 'Low Church'. Gary confirmed this by pointing out the lack of any smell of incense – usually a good indicator of a High Church place of worship. Our little pilgrimage group does like its incense. One year Gary even gave me a Christmas present of a bottle of aftershave called Incense, based on a Greek Orthodox smell!

As a little boy I was taken to visit cathedrals in England and France – Lincoln, St Pauls, Westminster Abbey, York Minster , Durham, Notre Dame, Rouen – and even at a young age appreciated that there was something very special about them. What I did not understand back then was that Scotland had its equivalents but that many of them had been destroyed since the days of the Scottish Reformation, with the exception of Glasgow and a few outliers, such St Magnus's Cathedral, Orkney. Even Iona has been virtually rebuilt from scratch in the last 90 years. I had been taught that there was nothing wrong with a cathedral being a ruin – that in fact this was some sort of advancement. I would beg to suggest that it was in fact an act of crass vandalism, the like of which was emulated by few other countries that had a Reformation.

Oban also boasts a lovely little shrine to St Columba with a delightful little icon. I collect icons but have never been able to find one of Columba for myself. I managed to resist the temptation of 'doing a Lord Elgin' and just trousering it from its sacred spot! If you visit, you should still see it there, unless of course someone else has made off with it by now.

From there we drove further north up the coast past Oban's Great Western Hotel and then Ganavan sands, another venue of happy memory for me. For many summers I and the 1982 year club from Glasgow University camped up and down the west coast of Scotland, generally getting into lots of bother and having lots of fun. On one occasion about fifty of us were camping on Ganavan sands. We had a few tents but the midges were so bad that most of us ended up sleeping in our cars. It was a contrast to our trip today – the fun was still there but on this occasion, not to sound holier than thou, we were genuinely seeking something other. I believe this seeking is in the nature of man, and gets stronger the shorter one thinks one may be around for.

Day 2

The next morning, following another hearty breakfast at our hotel, we embarked the ferry to Craignure, Isle of Mull, a short but pretty sail with plenty of rugged countryside to look at. Once onto Mull, however, the scenery changed quite dramatically. Soon after driving off the ferry the road thins down to just a single track for fifty miles. Mull is the Scottish Crete – an enormous island. There is, however, nobody there. One drives between mountains rising to between two and three thousand feet, with inland lochs, sea lochs and huge vistas. At Fionnphort at the south-west tip of the island one feels as if one has reached the edge of the world. The sand is white, the water opalescent green and there is a luminosity which is truly enchanting even in poor weather (the usual situation). At the ferry port for our crossing to Iona, I dropped Debs, Gary and Robert on the jetty with our bags before driving up to a free parking spot a five-minute walk away. When I returned on foot, they looked somewhat forlorn and wind-blown. The last time Deborah and I had taken this ferry she had looked much the same at this same point. 'Why have you brought me here? The weather is terrible, the place is miserable and are all these people religious nutters?' Once on the boat, however, crossing the sound of Iona, her mood had taken a 180 degree turn, and the same transformation occurred now for all three of my companions.

Having checked into the hotel on Iona and had a light lunch, we set off for the Abbey (via a second-hand bookstore) and then on to the island's Roman Catholic House of Prayer. This is a house containing a beautiful little church (although

Robert felt it too modern for him), and boasting some great icons of the Scottish saints Columba and Kentigern, also known as Mungo. The latter is the patron saint of Glasgow, his name associated with the Cathedral there and also the Royal Infirmary next door, which has the St Mungo Chair of Surgery.

That's not quite as good a chair as the Western Infirmary Chair – a Regius Chair that comes with an automatic knighthood, which even the London medical schools don't have. It is pretty difficult for doctors to get knighted these days. It was fairly common for doctors to be knighted from Victorian days through the first half of the twentieth century, but, as cure rates and the success of the profession rose, so our stock fell. I don't say this as sour grapes but as a reflection on what I think is a shallow wider society. If you win a medal for athletic achievement or kick a football well, hey presto you may well get knighted. I think that is great but feel sorry that others get left out. If you happened to have invented ultrasound (Ian Donald) or In Vitro Fertilisation (Patrick Steptoe and Robert Edwards), to name just two of the incredible achievements which daily help my patients and millions of other patients worldwide, you won't receive a similar honour. (Just recently, Edwards was awarded a Nobel Prize, although sadly he was too sick to receive it personally. Poor Steptoe has been dead many a year with no recognition – a poor state of affairs, I would suggest.)

After a short prayer in the prayer room, we walked over to the west coast for a swim. I say we – we all walked but only I had a swim, which probably suggests higher IQs for my wife and friends. Wow, was it invigorating though! We returned to the Argyll Hotel for a rest, followed by oysters and champagne, steak and salad, and much fun and laughter. Here lies the joy of all of this: the juxtaposition of serious intent with lots of fun. 'Centring' seems to be the modern phrase

– in other words, living in the in the here and now. The idea is to avoid the mundane and to try not to worry about the future, nor to dwell in the past, either good times or bad. This is not an easy thing to accomplish. However, I have no doubt that the practise of chant helps with this aim. Chant allows breathing, walking and heart rate to be in synchronisation with each other, and makes one feel amazing, with all life's little worries temporarily banished.

Ꝺay 3

Debs got up at seven o'clock and made a short visit to the Abbey by herself. She sometimes accuses me of religious zealotry, but this was a bit too disciplined for me the morning after the night before. Deborah is always saying that she does not like to be part of drinking culture, to which my reply is that she isn't – she is an observer of it. She married the wrong guy with the wrong friends not to be! We all made it up eventually though, and following breakfast we returned to the Abbey again as a group for its main morning service. The leader of the service, from the Iona Community, performed the service which involved dividing the congregation into those wearing jeans and those who were not, which seemed to come out at a fifty/fifty split.

Later that morning the four of us joined a boat trip to Fingal's Cave on the Isle of Staffa. This short voyage proved to be more sporting than it first appeared. Our boat was approximately forty feet long with a decent gunwhale, and as we appeared to have a fine if somewhat breezy day, Gary and I elected to sit at the back in the open air. Deborah and Robert went inside. When we left Iona there were no more than ten people on board but after crossing the Sound of Iona to Fionnphort, we took on board a large group of Scandinavian teenagers and their teachers. We were all offered oilskins, both coats and trousers, but Gary and I saw no real need for this although the disconsolate youth accepted the offer. With the boat now full we set sail northwards and, once the boat came out of the lee of the land, the sea started to become a little more … interesting. Gary and I were duly soaked by a large cold wave which crashed over the side. The teenagers had kept dry but some of them looked fairly green by the time we arrived at Staffa. I had shown a couple of them and their teacher the acupuncture anti-nausea spot (the application of firm pressure to the inner wrist in the central area) to apparent good effect, as none of them were physically sick at this point.

We arrived at a difficult little anchorage and disembarked, firstly visiting the cave, which is genuinely impressive. One can see why Mendelssohn was inspired to write his overture, and why Dr Johnson and James Boswell both waxed lyrical about it. I am a big fan of both of these men. Johnson said many things which are quotable but my two favourites are 'When a man is tired of London he is tired of living, for there is in London everything that life can afford' (my grandfather and uncles had this quote on their hotel brochures back in the sixties and seventies), and 'What is written without effort is in general read without pleasure' (so surely true, although hopefully not for you, dear reader since I have put a lot of effort in). He also made some fairly rude remarks about Scotland, along the lines of the best thing about it being the road to England. However, he was much more generous about Iona, writing that it would move even the least religious to some sense of this sentiment. As for Boswell, I have always related closely to him, having been given a copy of his London Diaries when I first moved to London as a qualified doctor. Boswell was the son of a Scottish judge, as am I. He moved to London to seek his fortune, as did I. He fell in with lots of interesting people, as have I. He, however, caught gonorrhea having copulated with a prostitute on London Bridge. Here I have avoided his lead, although in my first job in London I did treat a fair bit of it. I also have the distinction of being the only male doctor who looked after the West London prostitute group to be asked to their Christmas party – good fun and an entirely innocent event, I should make clear.

Iona - Day 3

Having seen the cave, we walked up the steps to the top of island and took in its splendid views of Mull, Iona, the Treshnish Isles, Rhum, Canna, Colinsay and, on the horizon, the Cuillins of Skye. Our hour on Staffa passed quickly and we re-embarked our boat. The trip back was much rougher and poor Robert needed to be velcroed to the toilet. He spent most of the journey in there. Some of the teenagers started to vomit, irrespective of acupuncture points.

After a light lunch back on Iona, Deborah and I set off on the Columba pilgrimage trail to St Columba's Bay. This is a three-mile walk south across the island traversing the island's golf course, (the most random course I have ever seen) and its reward at the end is of a splendid view of the bay, where Columba had come ashore bringing Christianity to Scotland for the first time (long before Augustine's mission to England and the foundation of Canterbury). The other contender for first Christian site is Whithorn in Dumfriesshire.

On the way back we walked along the west coast to Port Bhan, Iona's most famous bay and the one realised in the painting in my parents' drawing room. What a bay it is, with pink marble down either side, a pink marble rock island in the middle and pure white sand creating crystal-clear bluey-green water. A swim beckoned! It is important to note here that the ambient temperature was not exactly warm; the two of us were dressed in fleeces, and there was an elderly man on the beach in a long coat and heavy clothes. Debs and I stripped off and into our swimming gear and got straight in to the sea, and the elderly man stripped down to his boxers and joined us. He made a better job of it than we did, swimming much further and managing to stay in longer, and thanked us afterwards, saying that he had decided to abandon his planned swim until he saw us get in. Later that evening he brought his wife into the Argyll Hotel restaurant for her seventieth birthday dinner, and greeted us with an expression common in the hospital when one meets staff in their normal clothes outside the operating suite: 'It's great to meet you with your clothes on!' He hastily explained his joke to his wife.

Dinner on this occasion was a fairly fishy affair: haddock soup followed by mussels, haddock and couscous. With all these fish oils there was little chance of getting arthritis here on Iona. As a very small child I was taken by my parents to Easdale, in the West Highlands of Scotland, for my summer holidays, and visited the Reverend Ferguson of the United Free Church of Scotland. He was a great friend of my father and had been born and brought up in St Kilda prior to its evacuation (due to the decline of the inhabitants' self-sufficiency on this extremely inhospitable island) in 1930. Apparently there had been no arthritis on St Kilda because their staple diet comprised puffins, their eggs and fish. The Reverend Ferguson's daughter had achondroplasia, which used to be called dwarfism, and in fact provides me with my very earliest childhood memory. I can remember this rather strange but kindly woman looking at me in bed, and I was since told that I must have been only eighteen months old at the time.

Day 4

The following day, our last, we breakfasted at eight o'clock and then went to the service at nine. This time the leader divided us into those who had bread and those who had porridge for our breakfast, presumably because those were the food choices on offer in the Iona Community. We had had the same choice at the Argyll Hotel, although our bread or porridge was followed by a huge fry up! Before you think I am getting too smug, I should tell you that the waitress sadly dropped my breakfast on the floor and I so had a long wait for my feast. After the service we just had time before starting our journey home to visit St Columba's shrine, where Gary said a prayer and blessed a reliquary cross which I had bought and brought with me for this purpose. It was an old seventh- to ninth-century Byzantine Orthodox cross and there seemed to be a certain circularity about bringing it here to this centre of Celtic Christianity.

Iona so richly deserves its reputation. The thing which never ceases to surprise me is that, come rain or shine, and whatever one's mood while driving across Mull, as soon as the ferry starts to sail across the Sound of Iona smiles appear on everybody's faces. I spoke to a middle-aged man on the ferry as we returned and he asked me if it had been my first trip. I said no, and asked him the same question. He replied 'No, I've been many times. This place always makes me feel happy, in fact happier than anywhere else I ever go!' Well that sums it up, because Iona imparts the same feelings in me. It is the place which epitomises the Celtic phrase 'the thin place' – where one's senses have an over-riding feeling that one is close to something other than the physical world.

To quote Dr Johnson, 'That man is little to be envied … whose piety would not grow warmer among the ruins of Iona'. He wrote this when the place was in a state of ruination, and added: 'Perhaps in the revolutions of the world, Iona may sometime again be the instructress of the Western Regions'. How right and prescient was this remark, with all the good things coming these days from Iona and its community.

Chant

You may remember me describing in the Introduction to this book the time of my life at which I started attending a high church mass, and was both confirmed and my marriage to Deborah was blessed by Gary. I was very much enjoying the liturgy and spiritual connection that I found at church but I discovered that I had a real problem with the practice of prayer. The scientist in me struggled greatly with the concept of 'requesting' prayer. Why, if there was a God, should he be interested in my pathetic little problems? What constituted a big enough problem to justify a prayer from me, and what was I actually expecting to happen in response?

It was around this time that I was visiting Mowbrays, the Anglican bookshop, at that time just off London's Regent Street, and I happened across a little book called *The Way of a Pilgrim*, by an unnamed author. I've mentioned it once or twice already in this book so you may have guessed by now that it has a particular significance for me. In fact, this book was a revelation – a life-changing read. I still have my original copy; in it, I wrote 'Purchased 18/1/03 am', and below this 'Finished 18/1/03 11pm'! I have signed it off as having been re-read six times, but I have other copies too. I have also annotated in the front that I have given it to numerous friends over the years.

So what is so special about *The Way of a Pilgrim*? For me, the book demonstrates that mystical reality can be found in Christianity, just as much as it is present in Eastern religions such as Buddhist, Hinduism or Sufism. The book tells the tale of a man who has lost everything: his wife, his livelihood and his home. For good measure, he was physically handicapped and unable to perform manual work. He takes to wandering and on his travels he asks the clerics and others he meets, 'How do you pray?' None of the answers he receives are satisfactory, until he meets a monk who will become his *Starets*, his spiritual advisor. The *Starets* tells the wanderer that he needs to follow the advice of St Paul, 'to pray without ceasing', and then instructs him in this process which is based on the teachings in the *Philokalia*, an eighteenth-century Russian book which annotates the teachings of the Desert Fathers, those Christian monks who went into the desert from as far back as the fourth century.

Suddenly a method, the 'Way', of prayer – to pray without ceasing – is opened up for the reader. Certainly it was for me! The book quite rightly advises caution in starting the practice of praying without ceasing, and suggests in rather more words that one 'should not try this one at home' unless one has a spiritual advisor. I have heard Bishop Kallistos Ware, one of the foremost Eastern Orthodox theologians and co-translator of a modern English edition of the *Philokalia*, give similarly grave advice. I went to see Gary and asked whether he thought I should try it under his guidance, and he encouraged me.

The 'Way' as described in the book is a form of chant – a repetitive, contemplative prayer. The person praying uses a short phrase, such as 'Lord Jesus Christ have mercy on me' or 'Lord Jesus Christ have mercy on me, a sinner', which is known as the 'Prayer of the Heart'. This prayer is then chanted many times in repetition, perhaps a few hundred repeats at a time when one is first starting, but moving on to thousands as one becomes more experienced. Initially one is required to sit in a certain position while repeating the Prayer of the Heart, but as one becomes better practiced it can be done while walking. The chant is timed to synchronise with the rhythm of one's breathing, and then also with one's heartbeat, which I have found I can start to sense in my chest without needing to feel for my pulse. Now this may at first sound a bit meaningless, but if you get the hang of it over time you will know what I mean: gradually, as one chants, one feels one's consciousness moving into one's chest. I know that sounds a bit crazy but that is what happens. It generates a mystical sense of wellbeing, and any tiredness one is feeling seems to go away. If walking over long distances then one feels one could walk forever. The pilgrim in the *The Way of a Pilgrim* comments on this extensively.

You may have noticed that this sounds not dissimilar to the idea of a *mantra* in Eastern spiritual traditions. Most of the world's great religions have sects who chant – Christians, Jews, Sufi Muslims, Hindus and of course those who follow the Buddha – and while I'm not sufficiently qualified to comment on the other religions I think it's true to say that all believe that one achieves a form of wholeness (or is that holiness?) though the process. The Jewish chant is 'Lord God have mercy on me' as I understand it. The technique of mindfulness is one of the secular approaches to the same end. But it is the Christian method – this Prayer of the Heart – that works for me and which I feel most comfortable describing here, if only on the basis of my own personal experience.

I must stress again that I am not an expert, nor a spiritual advisor, and this book is not intended to be a 'how to' guide to chant or the Way or the Prayer of the Heart. There are dangers in entering into this practice unsupervised or without the wisdom of a guide. Do not undertake it lightly, and be prepared to become addicted to the Prayer – not necessarily a bad thing in itself but ultimately it could become self-defeating. In the novel *Franny and Zooey* by J. D. Salinger (by chance my daughter Victoria's favourite book – she introduced me to it!), Franny is a student who learns the Prayer in a secular fashion. With practice, she learns how to say 'Lord Jesus Christ' and 'Have mercy on me' in repetition in time with her breathing, and this develops as it should with the prayer moving from her head to her chest, and then to her heart as the words come in time with her heartbeat and breathing, so that ultimately she is no longer required to say the prayer aloud – it comes from within her. Franny finds all of this to be a pleasant experience but it ultimately becomes demotivating and harmful to her. Advisors from all religious traditions would probably agree that this is what one would expect to happen when the chant is practiced in complete isolation from its religious origins. The prayer should be used as part of a wider religious life rooted in liturgy and wise support. I think this also applies to the Eastern religions.

There is danger in becoming demotivated, but a greater danger in that one can arrive at a hallucinatory place where one is likely to over-interpret what one is seeing and experiencing. Historically this has proved to be a controversial issue for the Athonite monks who practice the Way, as some have accused them of not actually praying but rather sitting in self-induced trance-like states that are nothing to do with real prayer. Some of the monks claim that within this state they have seen 'unconstructed light' – a bright light that is not physical or of this world, but of heaven – which some critics have disputed as heretical.

Some might say that there is little difference between what I describe here as chant and hypnotic trance. I have quite a bit of experience in hypnotherapy, having been taught it first in 1983 in Stobhill Hospital in Glasgow and later having undergone deep hypnosis myself in the process of giving up smoking, and I know it has excellent medical application especially in the field of pain management. I also think hypnotherapy is great for 'rebooting' the brain when one's emotions are getting it wrong. We all go through times when the logical part of our brain knows we don't have a problem but our emotions are not giving us the same message and hypnosis can work really well here although not everyone is susceptible to it. However, the chant, I believe, takes one to a different place from hypnotic trance, and is better to help us live in the here and now.

I have no doubt at all that there is a spiritual dimension to all of this and accept that some things are beyond human understanding – faith would be meaningless if we could explain everything. However, there is rational science here too which fascinates me as a doctor, and I offer a brief explanation here for those who need further reassurance of the health benefits of chant and prayer through whatever religious tradition is right for you.

My friend and colleague Dr Tony Yardley-Jones is a consultant in occupational health and as part of his work on the scientific board of the Institute of HeartMath, with colleagues including Dr Rollin McCraty, has been researching heart rate variability, in particular in relation to the heart's response to, and creation of (in relationship with the brain), positive emotion. I was at a drinks party, in quiet but animated discussion with a hypnotherapist friend Shaun Hammond about the differences between prayer-induced chant and hypnotism-induced trance, when Tony overheard us and came over to tell us about a new device he was working on for the measurement of cardiac synchronicity.

The device – a non-invasive piece of technology derived from an ECG heart monitor – measures heart variability in response to different external stimuli and situations. At times of anger, high anxiety or agitation (which could be artificially stimulated by listening to, for example, Wagner's *Ride of the Valkyries*, although some with stress-filled lives may not need to do this!), the device measures a 'jaggedy' line of heart activity termed 'cardiac non-coherence':

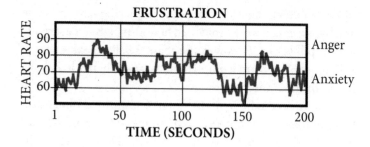

In contrast, the coherent heart responding to feelings of love, appreciation and compassion creates a calmer pattern known as 'sinusoidal'. This is the effect we get when seeing a beautiful sunset or perhaps listening to a piece of music by Bach or Mozart. I have listened to a lot of Bach while writing this book to keep me calm in the face of innumerable computer problems; his style of mathematically-composed music is popular among surgeons and anaesthetists for generating a calm atmosphere in theatre as an antidote to high anxiety situations. Similarly, other Baroque music which is quite technically complex has been proven to improve concentration in surgeons as it increases blood flow to the frontal cortex in the brain. It's probably not advisable to operate while listening to *Ride of the Valkyries*, mind you – it's no coincidence that this was used as part of the soundtrack of the war film *Apocalypse Now*! The 'Mozart effect' sinusoidal pattern looks like this:

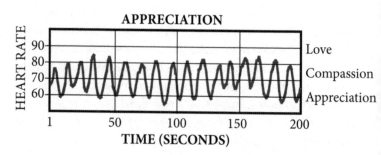

To some minds it may seem a bit outdated to view the heart as a centre of emotion. Traditionally this was the case, leading to the plethora of heart imagery we always see around St Valentine's Day, and it's perhaps telling that some Eastern religions describe *chakras* based on one's brain, face, heart and groin which relate to an intuitive understanding we all have about how we feel in different parts of our body (we talk about having a 'gut feeling', 'feeling it in my waters' or somebody having a 'big heart'). However, in the last hundred years or so science has come to believe that all emotion is felt in the brain and that we have a top-down structure by which the brain controls all the other organs, with those organs having effectively no input. But recent research is starting to turn some of these ideas upside-down and there is a better understanding of ways that the brain and the body work together to create thoughts and emotions.

In essence, the brain communicates with the organs of the body via neurological connections – transmissions down the spinal cord and out through the peripheral nerve network to all parts of the body – and also by the release of hormones from the pituitary gland. These hormones control a number of responses including, in women, ovarian function. What has become clear more recently is that the heart also signals to the brain and other parts of the body via the neurological system. In other words, the nerve conduction runs both ways – up and down the track! There is also biophysical communication via pulse waves, biochemical communication via hormones and energetic communication via electromagnetic fields. It turns out that all those Valentine's Day cards and songs about the heart may have more truth in them than we realized: the heart appears to have a very important role in the generation of emotion, and in fact in certain things the heart responds to external stimuli *before* the brain.

Chant, it seems, can lead from cardiac non-coherence

to cardiac coherence. After hooking my interest at the party, Tony turned up to see me in my office with his device, which he placed on my finger to measure my heart. Initially the trace started all jaggedy, which is what one would expect in the office, especially for me, but within a minute of my starting to chant the Prayer of the Heart it was showing the sinusoidal trace and I felt good within myself. I had been wondering whether the effects of chant were all in my head, but they are not, they are in my heart too.

A further proof of this came to me recently. I had been sent back to the cardiologist because of high blood pressure, notwithstanding the tablets I was already taking. He put me on the treadmill, I started walking and the faster I went, the lower my blood pressure became. This fits with how I feel when I'm walking and chanting inwardly at the same time: all tension dissipates. I now understand why high blood pressure gets called hyper-tension!

Of course we all attain cardiac coherence at various times in our life, although not normally for sustained periods of time as is the case, with beneficial effects thereafter, for those who chant. The research performed by HeartMath has demonstrated that the body has a sort of feedback mechanism, by which the brain becomes reprogrammed to maintain the positive feelings of cardiac coherence and to generate more of the same. Feelings of wellbeing and, most importantly, appreciation are maintained beyond sessions of positive feeling created for measurement by the heart monitoring device, and a positive circle is created. In studies, breast cancer patients have reported feeling more in control, more centred, happier living in the here and now and less depressed or worried about the future.

One of the amazing things about this new physiological research is how in tune it is with old intuitive ideas about how the body functions. What an irony it is that much of this learning has been around for thousands of years! Most of us know intuitively that positive thinking is a good thing but the HeartMath process is designed to generate positive feelings which appear to be longer lasting once engaged than thoughts alone. This isn't really the place for me to go into further detail but the website www.heartmath.com will tell you more about their story and ongoing research. Tony has also written a chapter of much greater detail about cardiac coherence in my book *Women's Cancers: Pathways to Living.*

This is the essence of why I have wanted to write this book. It is the first 'spiritual' book that I have written, after many medical ones, but as I hope you'll understand from what you have read in this chapter, I don't believe matters of the spirit should be considered mutually exclusive from matters of the body. The heart, perhaps, is the most obvious place to find both together.

It was a lecture that I gave to the Charing Cross Hospital Patients Association, on the subject of Doctor to Patient Communication, that emboldened me to write this book. My talk was initially concerned with a method of communication called the 'Four Cusps', relating to the four stages that patients with cancer go through (A = cured; B = 'living with cancer'; C = pre-terminal; D = dying; contrary to popular belief the vast majority of patients with cancer are either in cusps A or B at diagnosis, and very few are in C or D, certainly when dealing with gynaecological and breast cancers). I moved on to talk about the ranges of emotions associated with grief response, utilizing Dr Elisabeth Kübler-Ross' DABDA process (D = denial; A = anger; B = bewilderment/bargaining; D = depression; A = acceptance). There is a variant I use based on a construct of Gary's (who is chairman and founder of the Westminster Bereavement Association) called 'the landscape of grief', which adds an 'H' to the end of DABDA, standing for hope.

It was at this point in the evening that I decided I wanted to expand my talk a little, and so I asked the audience if they would indulge me for ten minutes while I introduced topics of spirituality and religion. The response was amazing. The up-until-now relatively quiet audience erupted. One woman shouted, 'This is what we want to talk about!' Another shouted, 'You and your bloody nurses won't talk to us about this! It's the most important thing!'

How have we ended up in a situation where doctors and nurses fear for their livelihood if they discuss matters of the spirit, yet in avoiding the subject are actually badly letting many people down? I understand that medical professionals should not proselytise just for the sake of their own religion, but preventing them being able to discuss these issues at all is just wrong. I believe that it is the militant atheists, of whom Richard Dawkins is the most well-known, who have all but shut down important discussions between doctors, nurses and patients. There are plenty of scientists, particularly physicists and mathematicians, who can easily reconcile their scientific knowledge with their religious beliefs yet the militant atheists suggest that only the unintelligent can have faith.

My own position is avowedly Christian and this book describes Christian pilgrimage simply because that is what I know about. It describes Christian prayer, again because that is what I know about, but it is not intended to be proscriptive and I hope it is clear to anybody reading this that those of any or no religion could reach the same place as that described by the path of chant.

Patmos

The day before, a little after midnight, 'I was in the isle which is called Patmos'. As dawn was breaking, I was in Chora. The sea was motionless and like metal bound the islands around. Not even a leaf breathed in the strengthening light. The peace was a shell without the slightest fracture. I remained transfixed by its influence; then I felt that I was whispering: 'Come and see ....'.

George Seferis

Day 1

For a number of reasons I was worried about making this trip, on which I planned to complete writing the manuscript of this very book you are reading now, and had been wondering whether it was the right thing for me to do. It would be the first pilgrimage lasting more than a day that I have undertaken on my own. I am gregarious by nature and went through my teens and twenties not much liking my own exclusive company, before having four children and a very busy professional and personal life which left me with little time to get used to being by myself. Additionally, this trip coincided with Deborah being away in New York with two of our friends so we had to leave the children in the ever capable hands of my sister, Alison, and her daughter Louise. One of my daughters, Madeleine, had a school entrance exam this weekend (we rationalised this worry by deciding that it was good to not be seen to be making a fuss over the test by cancelling either of our trips). Half-term is coming up. My workaholic side is feeling guilty about going away and telling me that I have not been in the NHS enough in the last few weeks to justify my existence. And, finally, three weeks ago I was admitted to hospital with localised peritonitis. Nevertheless, I decided that this was an important journey for me to take and so this morning Deborah and I travelled together to Heathrow, from where I caught my plane to Athens and she hers to the Big Apple.

Patmos is the island to which St John, writer of the fourth Gospel and three of the epistles, was exiled from Ephesus in 96AD by the Christian-persecuting Emperor Domitian, and on which the biblical book of Revelation, the last book of the New Testament, was revealed to him in visions which he dictated to the scribe Prochorus. John was the son of Zebedee and Salome, the sister of St Joseph. As a young man he and his elder brother James became fishermen, and were both called as disciples by Jesus. He was present at Christ's transfiguration on Mount Tabor, in the Garden of Gethsemane when Jesus was betrayed and it was he who reclined on Jesus' breast at the Last Supper. John was the only disciple to stay with Jesus all the way to Golgotha and, along with Mary, was present at his crucifixion. It was John who Jesus asked to look after his mother like a son, and John who was present when Thomas placed his hand in the side of Christ. His exile on Patmos ended after the assassination of Domitian and John returned to Ephesus where he would eventually die peacefully, the only disciple not to have been put to death.

History has little to tell us of Patmos after John left until St Christodoulos came to the island in the late eleventh and early twelfth centuries, having arranged for the island to be gifted to him and his monks by the Emperor Alexios I Komnenos. He founded the Monastery of St John the Theologian and began the work of preserving the cave in which John received his visions (now known as the Cave of the Apocalypse).

Having landed in Greece I decided to stow my suitcase and beloved walking sticks (Alpine poles from Megeve – much cheaper than Leki poles but more effective, especially with Greek dogs) at left luggage for a few hours to allow me to make a brief visit to downtown Athens. I was last in this area as a student in the late 1970s, when friends and I had stayed on the roof of a doss house off Syntagma Square. This time I looked less like a student and more a slightly strange tourist as I was pulling my airline pilot's style briefcase around with me. I didn't make it to the Parthenon but managed a quick wander around Plaka and a brief lunch before returning to the airport for my luggage and then heading on to Piraeus, from where my ferry to Patmos would depart. I had failed to realise that the airport and Piraeus were opposite ends of the line so I was having to cut back on myself in the wrong direction to get my suitcase and sticks. Fortunately I found George, a decent taxi driver waiting apart from the crowd of drivers hassling for business, who cut me a good deal for the whole round trip, drove as if he was in a Formula One race to get me to Piraeus on time and even found me the correct ticket office in the particular part of the huge port that my ferry was leaving from. I had paid for my tickets over the phone, with no email or any other kind of written confirmation of my booking, so felt a certain degree of anxiety as I handed over an old envelope with a reservation number on it. To my huge relief, the tickets were given to me with no aggravation and I struggled on to the ferry (helped with my heavy luggage by a kind Patmian in the queue) where I was shown to my cabin and – following some decent fare in the *à la carte* restaurant – was finally able to bunk down, at least until half past two in the morning when we were called with the announcement that Patmos was just twenty-five minutes away.

Day 2

I felt pretty disorientated when I disembarked and was initially disheartened to discover there were no taxis waiting at the rank, but it was not long before one showed up and whisked me off to my hotel in Grikos. To my surprise and pleasure, the proprietor, proprietrix and two of their staff had all stayed up to greet me on arrival, despite having to rise early later that morning to serve breakfast.

When I had made my bookings it had been difficult to determine exactly what sort of hotel I was going to be staying in: its own website looked brilliant but the island's website rated it only average, and Grikos itself was hardly mentioned in any of the guidebooks – it could have been the island's industrial centre for all I knew! But it turned out to be brilliant, and it transpired from my conversations with the owners that they simply hadn't been prepared to pay the back-handers required to get themselves an entry in the guides (my uncle's hotel in London was similarly under-rated). In addition, it would seem that some of the more competitive hotels on Patmos have bad mouthed them on the internet. Anyway, if you are going to Patmos, this hotel is the business. Pilgrimage lux! My only problem was that my mobile phone was defunct (I suspect the smooth talker from Vodafone who had phoned me a few weeks ago changed my tariff but neglected to include European connection in the new package), but perhaps this would turn out to be a blessing in disguise.

Waking the next morning at half past ten, I emerged from my room onto an external staircase and my nostrils were assailed with the wonderful smell of wild thyme. The

Patmos - Day 2

Greeks are so lucky to have such wonderful smells literally on their doorstep. In Scotland if you climb to high country in the summer you get the great smell of heather (although the incessant rain often puts a dampener on all country smells except cow shit), while in England one is sometimes lucky enough to get the smell of new mown hay.

After a superb breakfast I put my walking gear on and headed off in what I thought was the right direction. Naturally, I got it wrong again but in contrast to when Andrew and I set out from Spoleto, I did at least realise my mistake in just half a mile and not ten! The island is topographically confusing and it is easy at the start to get disorientated. What should have been a twenty-minute walk to Patmos's capital, Chora, took me an hour, but what a place I discovered when I got there. The town, about seven hundred feet above sea level, contains what seems like hundreds of churches, many of which are open for worship.

After a brief look around the monastery of St John (planning to visit it properly on a later day) I wandered past a number of the sorts of shops one expects to find at all mega-religious sites these days, although these were a bit classier than most, selling good icons instead of the usual tat. The main town seemed deserted, with all the restaurants closed apart from one I discovered with a fantastic view over Skala, called Jimmy's Balcony. There were a lot of Germans in town, plus a few French and Italians, and most of them seemed to be dining at Jimmy's. I was the only Scot, in fact the only person from the UK.

My return to Grikos along a hidden footpath that I had missed in the morning took the twenty minutes it was supposed to, allowing me time for a dip in the sea and then the hotel pool – both fairly cool by Greek standards but not by Scottish – before getting in a good six hours of writing either side of an excellent hotel dinner.

Day 3

Another day commenced with a superb breakfast – ham, eggs, homemade cheese pie and tomato juice, followed by croissants and coffee – before I set off on the road to Skala. What a wonderful walk in the sunshine it was, with the sea a deep blue giving way to green at the water's edge. There were a few boats about. Along the route there were many small chapels, some appearing to be private in people's gardens, while others were open, with candles lit and the wonderfully strong smell of incense coming from within. There was a bit of arable farming going on here near the coast as well as in the higher country. One fellow in welly boots was hoeing a field of vegetables by hand, which looked like hard work to me. It seemed to be very arid and there were obvious signs of artificial irrigation – not the sort of problem that afflicts the Scottish farmer. Later on, further up in the hills, I saw a lot of goats but the ground was dry with thorny bushes and there was no scope for cultivation. I guessed it was too rough for sheep, of which I did not see any, nor cows, although a good few donkeys were around, braying their heads off. It is amazing how much noise these little fellows make. How come horses don't make nearly the same noise? If Andrew were here he would no doubt have an explanation. I miss Andrew on these walks. We never talked much but walking with him was like walking with a naturalists' encyclopaedia: the trilling of birds, the buzzing of insects and the waving of wild flowers in the sunlight – Andrew could have told me what each of them was.

Skala itself is the main port of Patmos, a good anchorage

allowing big cruise ships to get in to disgorge their tourists in search of the island's sites. My parents are amongst those who have disembarked here. After some enquiries I found the start of the ancient cobbled path that leads from Skala up to Chora, past the Cave of the Apocalypse where St John received the visions that he recorded in what was to become the biblical book of Revelation. I was irritated to notice that two local youths seemed to be laughing at me (or was it with me? I doubt it, as I wasn't laughing), no doubt because I was already breaking sweat at the foot of the path. I probably looked a bit eccentric with my poles, back pack and blue-and-white striped scarf which I wrapped around my neck and then over my head, a bit like a turban. I have never understood how such a flimsy piece of material can reduce one's head temperature so dramatically. Yeah, I know the physics but it is still totally counterintuitive. The Glaswegian in me had a real desire to tell them to f*** off, and to clobber them with my steel-tipped stick, but the pilgrim in me was strong enough to realise that today – the big day on which I planned to take in the Cave and the monastery of St John before continuing my climb to the Prophet Elias monastery, the highest point on the island – was not the day to begin with a fight with the local youth. So I was a good boy and laughed along with them. I am getting better, I think. I hope!

My climb took me uphill on a cobbled track through a pine forest. About halfway up there was a narrow path off to my left, along which I rapidly found the monastic complex. On my visit it was a bit of a hotch-potch, with cement mixers lying around and not particularly suitable for photo opportunities. Above the complex sat the Patmian Ecclesiastical College, a modern-looking building in full use. I found the entrance to the Cave of the Apocalypse and walked in past an empty kiosk and shop where an old monk, who looked at me like I might contaminate him, was chatting to the shopkeeper. He motioned me downstairs where I met the only other 'walking pilgrim', a Greek grandma. The site is effectively a church – with a nave a good forty feet long and maybe twenty to thirty feet high with an *iconastasis* – bolted onto the side of an ancient cave. The church is that of St Ann, the mother of the Virgin Mary. She does not get much of a look-in in the West! For the record, her husband was called Joachim and the couple, along with the Virgin as a child, are often seen in an icon called the Presentation of the Virgin in the Temple.

The Cave has the appearance of a wave made of rock, varying between six and eight feet in height and with the facing wall covered with icons. Immediately this felt to me like a very holy place. It bore little resemblance to our caves back in Bute, which are a bit dirty and smelly thanks to pigeons. In one of the icons St John is shown seeing his vision of God with seven candles, which represent the seven ancient churches of Asia Minor. Below the figure of Christ, looking on this occasion extremely severe, is John, reclined and receiving his message. Next to this is an icon of John dictating his vision to his scribe Prochorus, who is writing it down fast and furiously. A further icon shows the Virgin. Beside this, to the right, is a hole in the side of the cave with a silver halo round it where John rested his head during his visions, and close is another silver-rimmed hole, marking the hand-hold where John helped himself up. The place where he placed his head is behind brass bars but you can easily put your hand through to touch this sacred place. The ground is made of rock which is fractured in three directions, by tradition a Trinitarian sign.

I descended a steep staircase to the church, where I found a doorman and three other pilgrims – two men and a woman – sitting on two bench pews. A few minutes after I joined them the woman got up and moved to some brass rails by the wall, where she lay down and against the side of the cave. Temporarily spoiling the prayerful atmosphere, the doorman then decided to move some boxes of candles about, and I wondered momentarily if he was creating a distraction out of annoyance at having seen me cross myself the Catholic way rather than the Orthodox way (Catholics make the horizontal motion from left to right, the Orthodox right to left), but I was just being paranoid. As I left later, having taken my turn on the floor to touch the hole in the cave wall (reminiscent of the hole where the cross was planted at Golgotha in Jerusalem) I shook the fellow's hand and he seemed to be perfectly friendly and decent man who had most probably just grown too used to the sanctity of this special place.

One of the reasons Patmos became a UNESCO world heritage site is that it is 'one of the few places that has evolved uninterrupted since the twelfth century. There are few other places in the world where religious ceremonies that date back to the early Christian times are still practised unchanged ... an exceptional example of a traditional Greek Orthodox pilgrimage centre of outstanding architectural interest'. Over the course of this and the several other pilgrimages I have made over the last few years I have become increasingly convinced that the Orthodox Christians, in their simple, long-held traditions, know a thing or two. Just a week before travelling to Patmos I had been having dinner with my friend Fr Anthony and we were talking about the Church's problems: all the sex scandals have been a disaster and I for one think that the Roman Catholics should follow the example of the Orthodox Church and allow their priests to marry. I know that there are plenty of celibate priests like Fr Anthony and Fr Gary who are happy that way but there have to be plenty who are not, which I am sure is a contributing factor towards all the trouble that has occurred. Another problem with Roman Catholic (and Anglican) churches are the persistent changes being wrought in their services and liturgies. In the Orthodox Church nothing changes, and one knows, when one partakes in their services, that one is part of a very ancient tradition. It is precisely the lack of change that makes the stories and traditions of Orthodox spirituality so believable. You may remember that having been in the Church of the Holy Sepulchre in Jerusalem, I was left in no doubt that I had been present at the true site of the cross. We questioned whether Pope Francis is moving forward in the right direction: there is no doubting that most of us like a grand ceremony (the grander the better for me, as you'll probably have noticed by now), but Francis has taken that name in order to look back to the values of St Francis, namely simplicity and closeness to the common man and woman, which is highly laudable. Will this work? Only time will tell.

My route back down the hill was enlivened by encounters with two sets of aggressive dogs – some big Alsatians which fortunately were chained up, but also some smaller, untied mongrels which ran into the road snarling at me. A wave of my stick and some good Glasgow expletives sent them packing, still growling, and I eventually arrived safely back at my hotel via a pine wood at its side. I had spotted a little church in the trees and went to look but found it shut, but from there I could see the hotel garden so I shimmied on down and climbed over into it, hoping not be seen by the owners. I managed a quick swim in the pool before settling down to work until midnight. Deborah and I finally got to speak by phone last night; the gap between Friday morning and Sunday evening was the longest since we have been together that we have not spoken. I have missed her a lot.

Day 4

The owners gave me a new room – an even bigger suite than the last one, with two rooms, a real desk at which to write, a balcony, a garden with Jacuzzi and a large bathroom. I made the mistake of asking the young, very attentive, Albanian member of staff who moved me there if this were the hotel's best room. He said no, that would be the Petra Suite. Unfortunately he then told the owner that I wanted to see the Petra suite, which I'm sure made me look plain greedy, but I never intended this! I told the proprietrix that I was very happy and had no desire to see anything else – oh, the difficulties of language.

However, I was able to put in most of a day of serious desk work, from before nine in the morning with no break until a quarter to three in the afternoon, at which point I pulled on my boots and went for a walk. I wore shorts – not suitable for visiting religious sites, but this was to be a day of being a walker and tourist. I walked south through Petra, about half an hour along a rough track over some hills and then down to a large cove to a beautiful beach called Psili Ammos. Apparently most people come to the beach on boat trips, not on foot. The walk had been very like the walk round Garroch Head on Bute – a rough track, on which one will meet far more goats (or sheep on Bute) than people, close to a monastic settlement (in ruins on Bute but very beautiful nonetheless) – but the similarities end upon reaching the sea: on Bute one arrives at the deserted and stunning Glencallum Bay where the sand is black and volcanic, the surrounding cliffs in hexagonal columns, but the water is freezing and usually plagued with jellyfish of the stinging variety (is there any other?). On Psili Ammos I found a Swiss couple and their young child who told me that they had been coming to this beach for fifteen years and it was the best on the island, which I could well believe. They left before long so I had the whole place to myself and had a swim in the beautiful water marvelling at what a fantastic place it was. I was a bit peckish after my dip and the only taverna on the beach was shut (it had closed the week before, according to the Swiss), but I was delighted to discover a packet of McVitie's All Butter Scottish Shortbread biscuits in the bottom of my rucksack, left over from when Debs had borrowed my rucksack earlier in the year!

I spent the rest of the day writing back at my desk, breaking at eight for dinner: a delicious veal in tomato sauce with pasta – some of the best meat I have ever had in Greece. I tried to buy the owners a drink but they refused and instead gave me a very large Metaxa brandy and showed me a beautiful book on Mount Athos written in this very hotel by a German author and photographer. It transpired that I am the third author to come here to complete a book and the very desk at which I am writing this now was bought for this very purpose – quite a privilege!

δαy 5

The day started early, or at least relatively so. I had been working to past midnight each night, but often waking with brain brimming over with things to write down and how to sort out this book once and for all. So this morning I rose at about eight and just started writing, with only one eye in proper focus! I had a quick but delicious breakfast of cheese pies, as only the Greeks can do them, with fried eggs and some pastries. The waitress always looks so upset that I don't want her fruit in the morning nor her salad in the evening.

After breakfast I worked through until half past twelve, at which point I changed into my walking pilgrim's gear, meaning that I was covered from head to foot with no flesh on display (a good thing in my case anyway!), and properly attired took the fast route straight up the hill track, arriving, lathered in sweat, in Chora within twenty minutes. I found the back route into the Monastery of St John the Divine, avoiding the kiosk (which was shut anyway), and located one of the ushers who was in mid-conversation with a kind woman from Athens called Penelope, the name of both my mother-in-law and a small boat which I have moored in Ithaca (a modest affair, I assure you: no sails or cabin, only a key and an engine, but it keeps the kids happy), although I did not appraise her of this as she offered to help translate my questions for the usher.

I must have had the appearance of just another sweaty, scruffy tourist but my reception improved when I produced a beautifully written envelope and letter of introduction kindly written for me by Metropolitan Kallistos, Bishop of Diokleia.

The Journey

I regret not keeping the letter, so lovely it was, but it had been designed for the abbot of the monastery and it did not seem right to request them back from his secretary. On production of the letter Penelope and I were taken by the usher to an office where two monks and a layman eyed me with some suspicion. The mood lightened when Penelope translated my letter and I was asked what I wanted, to which I replied that I would like admission to the afternoon Vespers. Was this all? 'Yes,' I answered, to the apparent surprise of everybody in the room, but it was true. I then said I had a present for the monastery – a copy of one of my earlier books, *Women's Cancers: Pathways to Healing*. This produced some amusement and interest, particularly when I showed them the book's section on cancer and spirituality.

The service was not until later in the afternoon so, with the atmosphere now more relaxed, they allowed me to stay at the monastery until then. A monk who turned out to be the abbot's secretary led us out onto the roof, offering fantastic views over the whole island. Penelope produced her camera and asked me to take many photos of her with the different views of Patmos as a backdrop. I learned that she was a pilgrim from Athens, and her good English stemmed from the fact that she was brought up in New England in the United States. Her husband was waiting for her and apparently becoming somewhat impatient at the time she was taking. I asked if he was on Jimmy's Balcony having a drink, but in fact he was waiting outside in the car. I get pretty agitated waiting in the car for Deborah, who I reckon is an amateur at the 'keep the husband waiting' game. I will try to be more tolerant in future!

Ten minutes before the service was due to begin a delightful elderly monk appeared across the courtyard, smiling at all and praying with his *komboscholi* (prayer beads). All the workmen smiled back and crossed themselves. He was generous to me, waving me into the church after the *semantron* (a large plank-like gong) had been beaten hard by a big, burly monk who carried it over his shoulder. The service was beautiful, the singing good. I know Byzantine Chant is an acquired taste! It lasted for half an hour, which is actually very short by Byzantine standards but just right today, and at the end of the service the monks and lay people venerated the main icons of St John the Divine and St Christodoulos' relics.

Besides Penelope and myself the only other lay person in attendance was a woman originally from Surrey, England, who had been in Patmos for the last thirty years or so and looked Greek and spoke perfect Greek, perhaps with a slight loss of English, although this may have been my ear, and she kindly kept me right during the Vespers. She had converted to Orthodoxy many years previously following a visit to the St Seraphim Chapel in Walsingham. In subsequent conversation, this lady and Penelope both demonstrated what I believe to be one of the few failings of the Orthodox Church – a complete lack of understanding of other Christian denominations. Penelope asked me if I was Roman Catholic, and I sensed my answer of 'yes' was not a popular one (I'm actually Anglo-Catholic, not Roman Catholic, but it has always seemed easier in this sort of circumstance to say the latter). I've experienced the same sort of thing many times on these trips of mine and have decided that the best response is to just nod and keep one's mouth firmly shut. Worse, to say one is an Anglican would be to prompt the question of whether one is actually a Christian. We are meant to be in Communion! One of the ironies here is that the head of the Anglican Church, Her Majesty The Queen, is married to Prince Philip, partly Greek and thus so is the Prince of Wales. The last Archbishop of Canterbury, Rowan Williams, wrote part of his thesis on Athos, and the Bishop of London, who very kindly wrote the Preface to this book, is a visitor to the Holy Mountain. Those of us at the bottom of the food chain need better press!

The Journey

After leaving the monastery I finally purchased a decent icon of St John and St Prochorus and, without asking, was given a great reduction and a free book on the Cave of the Apocalypse. I then realised my pedometer had run out of battery! *Quelle horreur!* I had been debating whether to go next to Skala or straight back to Petra, but this discovery persuaded me to head down the hill to Skala where I might find a shop for a new battery. Wrong decision! All the shops were shut and I had extended my walk by three miles, which had not been part of my plan for the day with so much work to do on the book. I had a Magnum ice cream and did the walk anyway, and just had time for a very brisk swim in the pool before returning to my desk.

Ꝺay 6

T his was the day that I finished writing the book … well, almost. I wrote today all day until after four in the afternoon, with no breaks apart from a quick but delicious breakfast around ten. This was also the last full day that I would spend on Patmos – I was due to head for home the next day – and I treated it as a non-religious day in my week of pilgrimage, locked away from the world – the Hermit of the Petra Hotel! The weather was overcast and threatening to rain, although at breakfast it had appeared less foreboding, with sun shining brightly through gaps in the clouds – the real West of Scotland look. With views of the island of Kalymnos in the distance, Kos beyond that and Leros a bit closer, it did feel to me very like the Western Isles. I commented to my hosts and their staff that this would be regarded as a fine day in the UK, which caused much amusement.

There were a lot of long faces around as there would be a lot of work to do if it was to rain. There were soft furnishings everywhere which would need to be put under cover. I am sure also that it was sad for the hotel staff to feel that another season was nearly over. They would re-open in March or April, which would mean a long gap with no guests. I have been very fortunate with the service I have received during my week alone, being waited upon hand and foot. The only other week I have ever spent alone was in New York, which was a very different experience; it is always said that cities are the loneliest places if you have no friends. But here at the Petra the staff were the most attentive I have ever encountered, even trying to get the wasps away from me by waving around plates with bits of sweet ham. Patmian wasps prefer ham to honey! Whenever I appeared back from my walks somebody was standing waiting for me with the key to my two rooms, balcony and bathroom. I have had all the books I have needed for reference and plenty of good music; it's no wonder my suitcase was so heavy!

Later in the afternoon I donned my shorts and t-shirt and decided to walk back to the amazing beach of Psili Ammos. As I walked along the track at the back of the beach near my hotel I suddenly become aware that there was a car behind me (I hadn't realised that I was on a road at all) which turned out to contain Penelope and her patient husband. They stopped, we shook hands and started to talk at some length. When I told them that I was here to write this book they asked the title and I told them what I had in mind for it at that point: *Walking, Chant and Pilgrimage: Pathways to Fitness and Fulfilment* (it changed eventually – my American patients had liked it as a title but it had not proved so popular with UK folks). When we had chatted the previous day Penelope had told me that she had sadly lost her mother to cancer and we had talked about the causes and so on. Now she asked me: 'Is this pilgrimage in pursuit of miracles?' Immediately I said 'No, my work is designed to help people live in the here and now, and improve their quality of life.' She nodded and said she thought that there was much need of something that could bring medicine and religion together. Then, in an act of great kindness, she jumped out of the car and gave me a handful of sweet biscuits – delicacies from Rhodes. I smiled because I had just been thinking that the taverna at the beach would be shut and although I had some water I had eaten all the shortbread, so I was worried I might get hungry. Penelope also told me about the service that took place every evening at the nunnery although I suspect I might not be welcome there!

I had left it too late to get to Psili Ammos so I turned

back towards Petra. My brain was whirling with thoughts of miracles, prompted by the words of Penelope. I have no doubt that miracles of the totally inexplicable variety do occur in life, although writing about them is not the principal purpose of this book. Most of the pilgrimage sites that I have described are not generally considered to be the healing type *per se*. In fact the only 'healing site' that I have been to is Walsingham, in the church of which there is a well where a service of the Sprinkling of the Holy Water takes place. My companions and I went to the well and had a drink from it on a silver ladle, were signed with the water in the shape of a cross on our foreheads and then had the water poured into our hands to be placed anywhere on our bodies that we had ailments. That for me suggested whole body immersion and a good dousing of my bank accounts in addition, but that was not an option so I chose instead to rub it onto my chest since I get asthma. The whole experience was profoundly moving, and for good measure I received a telephone call with some good news about my bank accounts in the car on the way home! This was not the sort of stuff that scientists are meant to get into at all. I do wonder if Carl Jung's theories about the collective subconscious may hold some weight here.

My walk back to the hotel took me past a huge rock I had been looking at for the last five days, away out to the right of the view from my room, and I saw a car driving out across the salt flats towards the rock and so I thought I would go and have a look. The car had parked up by the time I reached the rock and inside happened to be a kind fellow whom I had already met three times this week as he was the museum attendant at the monastery. He greeted me warmly and introduced me to his wife and their two young children in the back of the car. His wife had spent four years at the University of Stirling in Scotland, and quickly picked up on my accent. I was brought up only nine miles from Stirling. They told me a little bit about the rock and the disused hermitage it was meant to house, according to the guide book, and he showed me that there was a route round the rock which would not have been obvious to the uninitiated and that the hermit cave was high up – probably too high as we had just had some light rain and the climb seemed inadvisable.

Back at the hotel I was spoiled again by the staff who served me mozzarella cheese, ham and olives with my pre-dinner beer. Every night in the restaurant I had been reading *Words of Mercury* by Patrick Leigh Fermor. I love this man who made me laugh every night, and on this final evening I discovered that he was a fan of Friedrich Hölderlin, a poet who was obsessed with Patmos even though he never visited it. This is first couplet of his most famous poem, *Patmos*, describing his view of the Cave of the Apocalypse:

> *Near is the God*
> *And he is hard to hold*
> *But where there is danger*
> *There rises the Saviour*
>
> *Friedrich Hölderlin*

Thoughts at the End of the Journey

I hope that this book has helped you to see that there are many different paths to that which is denied by some, but deeply desired by many more. In each book of C S Lewis's *Chronicles of Narnia* series, the children find a different doorway from our world to the magical realm of Narnia: in *The Lion, the Witch and the Wardrobe*, it is through the back of a wardrobe; in *The Magician's Nephew* the transportation comes by touching magic rings; in *The Voyage of the 'Dawn Treader'* it is through a painting; and so on. The doorways are always unexpected and don't always work when or exactly how the children want them to, but they get them to where they really need to be.

This is how it has been for me in the journeys that I have described for you in this book. Each has had its own unique *modus operandi* and each has taken me to a very different place – spiritually and emotionally as well as geographically. But each has been the same in that on every journey I have been seeking to find a doorway. That seeking is much more important than the arriving. I fervently believe in the Celtic concept of the 'thin place', where one can get closer to God, and I have been fortunate enough to have found this more than once: in the wilds of Scotland, along the pilgrim routes of Assisi and Patmos, in some of the people I have met, and incredibly powerfully in certain cities – Jerusalem especially.

I urge you: go and explore for yourself. Have an adventure! Discover your own journeys.

Exercise is good on all levels, and I encourage you to walk more if you are able to. Walking makes us stronger, physically and mentally, and it releases endorphins – natural opiates which make us feel good and are highly addictive in the best possible way. Human beings were designed to walk, but the age of the car has encouraged all of us to spend more time travelling on our bottoms! If you take nothing else from this book, buy a pedometer and find out how many steps you are actually walking each day, not what you think you are doing. Remember: 10,000 steps, three times a week is the absolute minimum to aim for. If you are healthy you will not damage yourself in any way with this sort of regimen. Your joints will be fine, your muscles more toned, your cardiovascular system improved, your blood pressure lower and you will feel good. If you are going to walk long distances, buy yourself some walking poles, a platypus water bottle and a good pair of boots. The poles will make you go faster but will also reduce your chance of falling over and increase your upper body exercise. Finally in the event of encountering vicious curs they provide a great deterrent!

If you wish to learn chant, that's fantastic. Please: if you are Christian, do it within the context of a full liturgical life and with an experienced advisor such as your priest. If you are from a different tradition, you should again be sure to have an advisor. Persevere and you will find great peace and understanding.

Exercise and chant combined are a very powerful mix. Add to this the seeking and finding of a 'thin place' and you will have the icing on the cake.

'The dream is the small hidden door in the deepest and most intimate sanctum of the soul, which opens to primeval cosmic night that was soul long before there was conscious ego, and will be soul far beyond what a conscious ego could ever reach.'

Carl Gustav Jung,
The Meaning of Psychology for Modern Man

'Ask, and it shall be given you, seek, and ye shall find; knock and it shall be opened unto you.'

Matthew 7:7